Take
Charge
of
your **Life**

Take
Charge
of
your
Life

Unlocking Influence,
Wealth, & Power

JIM ROHN

An Official Nightingale-Conant Publication

Published and distributed by:
SOUND WISDOM
P.O. Box 310
Shippensburg, PA 17257-0310
717-530-2122

info@soundwisdom.com

www.soundwisdom.com

ISBN 13 TP: 978-1-64095-491-5

ISBN 13 eBook: 978-1-64095-492-2

For Worldwide Distribution, Printed in the U.S.A.

1 2 3 4 5 6 7 8 / 28 27 26 25 24

CONTENTS

FOREWORD

Ideas are life-changing. The ideas you grab hold of today and act upon can make all the difference in the fulfillment of your dreams. Just one good idea can take you to the top—and likewise, with a head full of wrong ideas, you can become permanently sidetracked from success. If you want to take charge of your life to really make the most of what it has to offer, Jim Rohn is the right man with the right ideas.

Jim knows the secrets of success. He devoted his life to a study of the fundamentals of human behavior and personal motivation that can awaken a remarkable power for achievement in you. With his unique style of philosophy, wisdom, wit, and solid common sense, he provides practical information and motivation from which you will profit.

In this book you will discover the five pieces of the life puzzle, which is a body of knowledge guaranteed to help you achieve your greatest goals. You will learn the success secrets of an effective communicator and learn the leadership skills needed to get ahead in whatever you set your mind to achieve in life.

Jim Rohn has an international reputation as a dynamic, effective public speaker—conducting workshops on personal development worldwide. Jim credits much of his success to the teachings of his mentor, Earl Shoaff, mentioned throughout the book.

There's power in the touch of human words—may what you read bring you much satisfaction, self-awareness, and the seedbed of great success in every aspect of your life.

Nightingale-Conant Corporation

1

PERTINENT PRELIMINARIES

Some people have an incredible zest for life and an appetite for living well and doing well, and others seem to have a ho-hum attitude to let it slide and hope it'll work out anyway. I don't know what makes the difference in people, but I've always found it exciting to watch people who are inspired to make the best of life. Self-motivation is key to overcoming challenges and difficulties.

Life is a challenge, which is no surprise to anyone. Therefore, it is so important to articulate the challenge, the press, the push—because the push is on, daily. Yet that's what life is all about—accepting the challenge, driving the roots deep, becoming as strong as possible, accepting everything that comes and making it into what you want to make it, attempting your best, trying your hardest, thinking well, reading well, living well, and struggling with it all. *That's the challenge—and that's what makes life worthwhile, that's where the value is, the struggle for high ideals to make something unique out of your life.*

One of the greatest experiences anyone can have is the experience of influence, to persuade somebody that we have a good idea, to persuade somebody to buy a product or consider a service, to be able to influence somebody to a way of life, an idea, a company, business, or enterprise.

INFLUENCE

Influence is one of the greatest of life's experiences—the chance to influence others, their thinking, their future, maybe their lives. All the way from being a manager to an executive, to being a parent, we all have, in some respects, the chance and the opportunity to influence somebody else.

Becoming an influencer can be accomplished casually, haphazardly, or on purpose by learning the skills. That's what I cover in this book—gathering the skills to help influence people to a way of thinking, to a product, to an idea, to an enterprise, or just to a better life—the skills of leadership.

The following is a list of three preliminary skills that lead directly to the five puzzle pieces of life that are identified and discussed throughout the book:

1. Sincerity

2. Ideas

3. Inspiration

Number one is *sincerity*. To accomplish anything important or of value, we have to start with sincerity. I would assume you're sincere in your intent to learn how to take charge of your life or you wouldn't be reading this book. You wouldn't have made the effort and pushed past whatever you had to do to get to the place of taking the time to read what I have to say, and I can appreciate that. Always start with sincerity. Hopefully you'll find me sincere in bringing value for your time and effort and consideration.

Sincerity is not a test of truth, though. We must not make the mistake of saying someone's right just because the person is so sincere. It's possible to be sincerely wrong. Hopefully you'll find me both sincere and truthful, but you have to decide for yourself what is truth. Here's the key—weigh sincerity on sincerity scales and weigh truth on truth scales. Don't weigh truth on sincerity scales.

IDEAS PLUS INSPIRATION

If you want your life to change for the better, here's the source of it all—*ideas plus inspiration*. Ideas are not that far away. In fact, I have a good phrase for you to consider that will serve you well for the rest of your life: *Everything you need is within reach*. The ideas you need for life change or business change is within reading reach and within listening reach.

There's probably a library not too far from you. The problem is, most people drive right by libraries, very few stop, park, and venture in. "Poor" Andrew Carnegie set up many libraries across the country thinking everybody would stop by and take advantage of all the books and knowledge within. He thought surely they would stop. [Between the library and the Internet, no one today has any excuse for not being able to learn what they need to know to get ahead.]

The key is to reach. Reach out and read, learn, meet people, experience new adventures in life, find the key to your future.

Everything you need is within reach.

There's a simple Bible phrase that says if you search, you will find. It's very important to know that finding is reserved for the searchers. We don't find what we need, we find what we search for. Needing is not the prerequisite to getting value. You can't be a needer, you have to be a searcher. But if you search, if you try, if you go, if you listen, ideas are within reach and ideas are life-changing. There's nothing so powerful as an idea whose time has come.

A business idea, social idea, an investment idea, good health idea—all you need is the refinement of an idea to make an impact on your life. Gather treasure, gather equity, gather wealth, because it doesn't take much to make a significant difference as the time passes. You might draw a little circle on a piece of paper and mark it that this is where you are now. Ten years from now, you could be 1 inch or 6 inches away from that first mark. The difference in ten years between here and there could be significant in terms of money and lifestyle, treasures, equity. In ten years there can be an *incredible* difference—if you make even a *small* change of discipline and thinking to start you on the journey of a lifetime of achievements.

GATHERING TREASURE

It's also very important intellectually to know whether or not you're headed in the right direction. Thinking about and deciding your direction now will lead you to gather intellectual and personal and spiritual and moral and economic treasure along the way. The key is to start today making changes to walk this new road. And here's what's exciting to me. Making just a few daily changes in disciplines will make a great deal of difference in one year, three years, five years, and definitely ten years. That's what you will learn throughout the book—the few daily disciplines that make the difference whether you wind up where you started or at the end of an exciting and profitable ongoing journey.

Ten years from now, you will surely arrive. The question is, *where?* We don't want to kid ourselves about where we will arrive or about the road we're walking to get there.

When I was in my mid-twenties, I had a "Do Not Kid Myself Anymore" day. I didn't want to go through life disillusioned anymore. I was just crossing my fingers and hoping for the best, but finally decided that theory would not get me what I wanted, that isn't where the treasure lies. I had to make sure I was on the right path. I needed to add disciplines to my life: a few reading disciplines, disciplines of mind, and a few disciplines of activity—and then I knew my path was safe and secure and I was walking toward my destiny. Only a few changes made all the difference!

Sometimes we get the idea that we're only doing about 10 percent of what needs to be done, and there is about 90 percent more that we need to do to make the difference for our fortune. Yet the opposite is probably true. You're doing enough to have arrived here today. You're doing enough to have bought and shared in the good life so far. So maybe all you need is that extra 5 or 10 percent of intellectual change, activity change, a refinement of discipline, a refinement of thought, and the ideas to make those simple changes. Then the equity starts gathering in year one and continues through year three, five, and ten!

I have a good comment for you to note: *Now's the time to fix the next ten years.* Sometimes you have to come to grips with reality and with truth.

When I met Mr. John Shoaff, I was 25 years old, he was 44 years old, and he brought me a wealth of experience. He asked me the tough questions, big questions, such as, "Are you reading the books that will take you where you want to go in the next five years?" An excellent question that you want to ask yourself. To get to where you want to be in the next five years, you're either reading the right books or you're not. That's a brilliant statement. You're either engaged in the disciplines or you're not.

Here's what we *don't* want to engage in: disillusion, hoping without acting, wishing without doing. The key is to take a good look at your life and ask, "Where am I? What can I do to make the changes necessary to ensure that I'm taking specific daily steps toward the treasure I want—the mental treasure, the personal treasure, the spiritual treasure, the financial

Now's the time to fix the next ten years.

treasure. I don't want to make any errors. Now's the time to adjust my daily program to take me where I want to go."

I have ideas to share to help you make a few powerful adjustments. Over the decades of lecturing, I received many letters and some personal testimonies from people who have experienced remarkable achievements by using just a few of my suggestions. This is definitely worth taking the time to read and learn. I'm here to do a little coaching.

A good note: *We can all use a little coaching*. When playing a game, it's sometimes hard to see all the moving pieces—but the goal is to win while doing your best. If we just sit and take a breather once in a while, take a little time out, we are refreshed and can head out again on our journey with renewed vigor. That's precisely what you're doing here now, reading this book.

Take a little time to listen to someone's experiences. As I share with you my experiences and ideas, see if it might cause for you a little moment of correction, so that you can make some changes that add up to some extra worth in the next one, three, five years. All kinds of ideas about health, enterprise, living the better life, and primarily, skills of leadership.

INSPIRATION

The next key word is *inspiration*. Inspiration is a mystery. Why are some people inspired and others are not? Personal inspiration can be defined as drawing emotional vitality from life and the challenge and going for it. We all admire that. Hopefully you'll find and become inspired as we study together.

I belong to a group that does business around the world. We've discovered a lot of ways and means and methods and ideas. As I share those exciting aspects of my life with you, I hope they serve as guidelines that translate a response into results.

I don't know where I've caught you during this time in life. Maybe this is springtime for you; you have a new opportunity and there's no telling what you're going to make of it. You're all excited. I congratulate you for that. Maybe you've been caught during harvesttime and you're celebrating your success.

Maybe this is summertime for you when sometimes the going is tough and the weeds are attacking your garden and the bugs are after your values. Summertime is an interesting time. It's not that easy to last from spring till fall. Summer's a test and especially when the creditors are calling. We have a tendency to walk out in the field and say, "Grow, crop, grow. There are demands on me." Or maybe you're caught in a testing time, a challenging time.

Maybe I've caught you in winter. We've all had desperate, decision-making winter times. Maybe you're at the fork in the road and some of the decisions you make in the immediate future will have a significant impact and everything to do with your next five to ten years.

I've been to a few of those so-called forks in the road. Which way do you go? What do you select now as your next path of opportunity? Maybe these are trying times for you. Winter can be a source of trial when you feel the push and pressure.

I don't know where I've caught you, but whatever season you're experiencing, I want to bring you value and a sense of direction so you can take charge of your life. That's my intent.

BE…

To get the most from this book, let me give you a quick list of how you can take advantage of all that you have going for you—right now, just as you are.

BE THANKFUL

Here's number one. *Be thankful.* I think, first of all, to get more we need to be thankful for what we already have, especially living in this unbelievable country. The average working person in the United States of America makes more than people in most of the world. We're such a rich, fabulous country.

It's unbelievable. [Median household annual income in the US in 2022 was $54,000 and in neighboring Mexico it was $18,000. In Bangladesh it was $245.] I'm sure they would find it strange that people would attend lectures and read books on how to do better when we're doing better than the majority worldwide.

I gave a lecture one weekend at our ranch in Clear Lake, California, for a nice group of people. I arrived a little early before the Friday evening session and was surprised at what I saw in the parking area. Cadillac El Dorados and Continentals and Mercedes and Ferraris and one Rolls-Royce, unbelievable. I walk in and here's this good-looking crowd and my opening remarks were, "Ladies and gentlemen, I think the rest of the world would find it strange that we have all come here this weekend to try to figure out how to do better. Surely the rest of the world would say, 'I don't understand.' But the man in

Be thankful for where you are and what you already have.

his Rolls-Royce may be saying, 'I have to get to the seminar to find out how to get another one of these.'" Incredible.

But here we are, probably doing very well. So let's be thankful for where we are because that's how good ideas start to flow, thanksgiving for what we already have.

What blocks the flow of all good information? Cynicism. It's not that difficult to be a practiced cynic, feeling cynical about circumstances, cynical about places, cynical about opportunities, cynical about people—it's easy to complain. But if we turn cynicism into thanksgiving, now the ideas can flow, information can flow, refinement of ideas can flow. That's number one, be thankful.

BE EAGER TO LEARN

Here's number two. *Be eager to learn*. No matter what you know, there's always more to know. A point I'd like to make here is that when I have time in the lectures, I like to argue it all out. I like that format. There's nothing like a good powerful discussion to learn how to refine an idea. What we want is ideas that pass the test of the tough questions, and it's good to be around people who can ask the tough questions. Debate has a unique way of refining ideas and that can become a valuable learning tool. It's beneficial.

I ask you to argue with all this that I'm discussing later. Go back over your notes and relive the experience and think about what you've read and what I've shared with you here. *The key is to stimulate the mind, to think thoughts and to think ideas, to open channels of information.* Refinement of intellect is where the future fortune lies—so be eager to learn.

BE A GOOD LISTENER

The last admonition is to *be a good listener,* which isn't easy these days. Everybody wants our attention. Radio voices and television voices and advertising voices and political voices and social voices and religious voices and community voices and family voices—how do you sort through all the voices and give extra time to a voice of substance? It isn't easy.

But if you practice the art of good listening, there is no telling what you can find in the way of ideas that can help change your life.

2

FIVE PUZZLE PIECES OF LIFE

All right, that's enough of the fundamental preliminaries. Now, let me give you the five major pieces to the life puzzle.

One time I was asked, "If somebody needed help, could you identify in what areas of their life they needed change, and could you categorize that into some simple steps for them to take?"

I said, "Yes."

I came up with the five major pieces to the life puzzle. At one time or another, we all need help in one of the following five areas or pieces. I'm sure you can guess what they are:

1. Philosophy

2. Attitude

3. Activity

4. Results

5. Lifestyle

Let's look at each one in detail.

PHILOSOPHY

Number one is philosophy. *Philosophy is simply what you know.* Now, to correct a couple of old cliches, what you don't know *will* hurt you; and to correct another one, ignorance is *not* bliss. It's so important to have the correct philosophy. It's so important to *know.* Philosophy sets the course of your life. It is the major piece in the five major pieces of the life puzzle.

Many other things are minor, some just don't affect your life that much—but these are five areas that affect our lives immensely.

I tell students during my lectures, "Make sure you get all the information you can while you're in school. I know it's laborious, I know it isn't easy to read the books and take the classes and try to get good grades, but hey, while you're here, gather it all up. because there's nothing worse than being stupid, right? Being broke is bad, but being stupid is awful."

To correct all that, we come back to number one. You have to *know,* because what you *don't know* will definitely affect your economic future. The book you miss reading will make a difference. The information you don't have will make a difference in the legacy of your equities over the next few months, the next few years.

Philosophy is where it all begins.

I divide philosophy into three parts:

One is basic, *starting-out philosophy.* The baby starts processing information right away. Cold is bad, warm is good,

Your philosophy of life is where it all begins.

hungry is awful, food is terrific. The baby starts reacting and processing information and having certain reactions to it. Our philosophy starts early, gathering information and reacting to it.

Next is *expanded philosophy*. This is when we have at least enough philosophy to be gainfully employed and offer a value to society, find our place in the marketplace, and be a reasonable decent human being. This is expanded philosophy.

But now, how do you become wealthy and powerful, sophisticated, influential, and unique? Simple, *refined philosophy*, which means extra studies and extra books, extra classes and thinking, extra pondering, the extra give and take of testing ideas and debate and discussion. All that is where the extra life comes from in the dimensions of refined philosophy, the extra thinking.

These are the steps of intellectual discovery that a lot of people just don't want to take or they're too busy to take. Or they present themselves in too strong and tough a manner, these extra skills that make all the difference in the outcome. But I'm telling you, once you start engaging in these extra skills, you will never want to go back. This new intellectual discovery is where the wealth is, where the happiness is, the good life, influence, power—refinement of philosophy.

Our philosophy comes from a lot of places—teaching, the influence of others, the books we read, the classes we take. You might want to underline the word *influence*. This is where a big share of our philosophy comes from, other people's influence.

When considering how you came to your current philosophy of life, there are several important questions to ask yourself. The big major questions to ask:

- *Who are the people I'm with the most?*
- *How are they influencing me?*
- *Am I going the right direction when I'm with them?*
- *Are they reading what I should be reading?*
- *Do they think about what I need to be thinking?*
- *Am I saying what they are saying?*
- *Am I becoming what they are or what I should become?* (The big biggie question.)

Influence plays a major role in the development of our philosophy. How we think, how we speak, the formulation of ideas, the things we weigh concerning values—all of this is so very important. What we know, the mind, thinking, processing ideas and information is the basis of us as human beings.

Ideas are simply information taking form, and the whole process of mind and thinking and knowing and processing ideas and information is of great magnitude because it determines the major piece of the five pieces of the life puzzle, your philosophy.

We all do something very important with what we know, we weigh it. We put it on our mental scales and weigh it. We may give it a number from 1 to 10, probably not consciously, but if we hear something and we come into possession of some information, we may give it a 10 and will act on it right away. If we give it a 1, we'll probably let it slide. If it's important, we'll do something about it. If we don't think it's important, we'll probably let it go.

Thinking, ideas, processing, knowing...

After receiving information, it's vital to *evaluate,* a key word we learn in leadership skill training. We need to evaluate the information to try to find value, perceived or anticipated. Where is the value? How valuable is it? How important is it? Is there something that I can't see at first glance? Is there value below the surface? In the inner workings? What goes behind it? What goes beyond it? What is its origin? All of these questions help us come to the perception or gives us insight for how to value ideas and evaluate information.

We must have a good set of mental scales. What if in processing information your mental scales were off-balance, and you weighed everything a little wrong? Do you think that resulting philosophy would affect your life? The answer is yes, of course. If you are just a little off over the course of 10 years, you can imagine what a big difference that would become. A key phrase for you regarding this perpetuation—*life accumulates.*

Life accumulates.

We either accumulate the debt or the value. We either accumulate the regret or we accumulate the equity. We must all suffer one of two pains—the pain of discipline or the pain of regret. I'm suggesting discipline, mental discipline to refine ideas. Of course, it's laborious, and of course, it makes us push, but it's a small price to pay so we won't have the pain of regret later on.

Regret weighs tons. Discipline weighs ounces.

If you accept the early ounces of discipline of thought to refine ideas and not let major questions pass you by, what about the possibilities for involvement you may miss? What about business? What about your value and your place and your future? What about your life? What about origin? What about destiny? What about opportunity? And even larger questions: What about society? What about government? What about religion? What about capital? What about education? What about world affairs? What about life?

All of these are major questions that need to be answered. To let them go casually by without a thought is to miss the treasures that your life could accumulate and absorb in the coming months, the coming years. These are issues and concerns that we need to ponder and what we must think about that sets the course of our life. Each one helps set the sail that takes us farther along on the journey to our desired destination.

Here is a good question to write down or at least underline here in the book. *Where are my thoughts taking me?* This is a biggie question. You can be casual about some minor areas in your life, but some things must be taken seriously. Your philosophy is taking you somewhere—either somewhere positive or somewhere negative. Big question—where are

Where are my thoughts taking me?

your thoughts taking you? The accumulation of equity will either be there or won't be there—life accumulates. You're either accumulating debt that you'll be sorry for or you are accumulating value that you'll be happy about.

Okay, so philosophy is the first major piece in the five major pieces. Next is attitude.

ATTITUDE

Number two is attitude. *Attitude is how you feel.* First of all, we're affected by what we know. Second, we're affected by how we feel about what we know.

Attitude is the emotional part of the five major puzzle pieces; and the question is, "How do I feel?"

There are many different ways to feel, and accompanying attitudes. For example, someone may say, "If this is all they pay, I'm not coming early and I'm not staying late on the job." We call that one way to feel. That's the person's choice of attitude. If that worker kept that attitude for the next five years, would it greatly affect his or her fortunes?

The answer is, of course, yes, it would affect promotions, bonuses, even retention.

You cannot escape the accumulated effect of your attitude. You can't escape it. A major question to ask yourself: *"How do I feel and am I on track or off track regarding my attitude?"* Attitudes are not always easy to fix; it's not easy to get information about how to change a bad attitude. It's hard to look up attitude in the yellow pages. If you could put your car in the shop and go next door and get your attitude tuned, wouldn't that be nice, right?

So where do you go? How do we engage in the kind of philosophical thinking that will refine our attitude to give us a chance for future fortune rather than what will be missing in the future? This is big—attitude.

Here's another attitude using the same scenario. "No matter what they pay, I always come early and I always stay late to invest in my own future." Why does one person have a positive attitude and another person have the opposite attitude? We call that mysteries of the mind. I don't know. Everybody has to choose for themselves. Attitude can change decisions through education. For instance, if you didn't know what the consequences were going to be (bad attitude equals termination), it could be very easy to choose the wrong attitude and not discipline yourself to the right attitude.

Adopt an attitude for a future fortune.

A large portion of our life is affected by how we feel. The following is a brief list about the feelings that affect our lives. Number one is *how you feel about the past*. It's so easy to carry the past as a burden instead of as a school from which to learn. It's easy to let the past overwhelm you instead of allowing the past to instruct you. How you feel about past hurts and past losses and past difficulties and the times you failed and the times that didn't work—the accumulation of all of that will greatly affect your future.

Number two is another major factor that affects your life—*how you feel about the future*. Our life is affected by *price and promise;* it's not that easy to pay the price if you can't see the promise. I think kids are having problems these days trying to pay the price because they can't see the promise. But all of us wouldn't mind paying the price if we could have a clear view of tomorrow, next week, next month, next year.

If we had the high assurance with great probability of how something is going to work out, do you think we would hesitate to pay? The answer is no, but everybody hesitates to pay if the future isn't clear. To help kids these days, we have to do two things: help them see the promise and help them pay the price. Be there to support them through the rough times.

Adults too—we will pay if we can see the promised result.

My karate instructor said, "Mr. Rohn, you can't believe the incredible feeling of walking down any city street unafraid." I said, "Let's get on with the classes. Hey, I will sweat. I'll put myself through the paces!"

What would we do for an extraordinary promise? The answer, the most unbelievable things. Would you crack the books open? Would you burn the midnight oil? Would you engage in the extra thoughts and the extra disciplines

The price for the promise.

if the promise was adequate? The answer is, of course. But who wants to read, who wants to burn the midnight oil, who wants to put themselves through the paces if the promise isn't clear? Not many. Important—price and promise.

Number three is *how you feel about each other*. Your attitude about society, country, state and city, community, family, enterprise, office, company, corporation, division is important. Taking charge of your life includes having a unique understanding about other human beings and how you feel about them. What constitutes a good life? Your attitude and how you feel about others.

I have another good phrase for you: *you can't succeed by yourself, so to have a unique refined sense of appreciation for each other is a prerequisite*. It takes each other to build a society. It takes all of us to build a country, to build a nation.

You can't succeed by yourself.

It takes all of us to build a community. Key phrase, you can't succeed by yourself.

I gave a speech to the Rotary Club of Culver City, California, and I was unusually affected by the Pledge of Allegiance that day. Big strong voices, it's a big strong club. The sound of the words was going through my mind the next few days, the Pledge of Allegiance, and the more I thought about it, the more I thought, *What an important key document! The Pledge of Allegiance*. I started writing and wrote a discourse on the Pledge of Allegiance. I took each keyword and summarized it for our tape of the month club.

Wow—it was an incredible exercise in receiving information and then refining it to expand my philosophy! The Pledge of Allegiance is unique. It starts with "I" and ends with "all." It takes all of us to make any one of us successful, and a unique refined appreciation of the *all of us* is what makes the I of us do much better. That appreciation of society, it takes all of us to make a market. We need each other's ideas and inspiration. Once you have that sense of appreciation of the all of us, now, you and your place and your possibilities and your opportunities start to really soar when you understand how important it is within the framework of the all of us. You can't succeed by yourself. It's hard to find a rich hermit.

Now here's the big biggie. *How you feel about yourself is major*. Understanding self-worth is the beginning of progress. How valuable are you? What could you do if you had all the skills? If you took the extra classes and burned the midnight oil, what could you do? What true value could you become?

This is one of the best exercises; ask yourself:

- *What could I become in terms of value?*

- *What could I really do in the marketplace, in enterprise, family, home, love, experience, marriage, friendship?*

- *How valuable could I become?*

- *Am I valuable enough to work on what all is still not functioning in my life to full capacity?*

- *If I'm operating at 20 percent, what could I possibly do with the other 80 percent, and do I have it in knowledge and worth and value and experience?*

Once you start understanding this part of you, understanding how valuable you are, it is a whole new experience, understanding self-worth is crucial to living with a positive outlook. Attitude plays a major part in how your life works out.

ACTIVITY

Number one is *philosophy.* Number two is *attitude.* Number three is *activity. Activity is what you do.* Our lives, first of all, are affected by what we know. Second, our lives are affected by how we feel. Third, our lives are affected by what we do. It is so important to understand these key puzzle pieces.

If you want to influence and help people, success is doing. You have to actually *do* it. Activity is a high priority in the life process to receive maximum benefit from what is available.

The following are important questions for you to answer.

- What is your philosophy about activity?

- What about hard work?
- What about long hours?
- What about full days?
- If you're doing something, how hard should you go at it?
- How much time should you put in?

Everybody has to develop their philosophy about activity. By way of review, think back over the past week and consider these questions.

A quote from the Old Testament says, "Six days activity, one day rest." That's called a *philosophy of ratio of activity*. What is a good ratio of rest and activity to you? Maybe 6 and 1 is too old a philosophy? Maybe five and two is better? I don't know.

We all have a philosophy about activity, which affects the rest of your life. Not to think so is naive. A good clue: unrest make rest a necessity, not an objective. The reason for life is enterprise. The reason for life is productivity. The reason for life is to see what we can do with the seasons and the chances and our mind and our spirit selves. That's what life is all about, to see what you can do.

Now you need to establish a philosophy on how much time you're going to spend doing. I've decided that enterprise is better than ease. If you rest too long, the weeds take over the garden in the summer, so you can't rest too long.

Life doesn't stand still and the threat of unwanted aspects of life will start overwhelming the good values of life if you just let it go. Let me give you one of the best philosophies I know in regard to activity. An ancient phrase says, "Whatever your hands find to do, do it with all your might." That's

Life is all about seeing what you can do.

a philosophy. You may say, "Well, I'm getting by with half my might." Well, that may be okay for you for a while, but if you decide that is going to be your own personal philosophy of activity, be ready for the negative consequences.

This philosophy I just mentioned says to do your doing with all your might. Do you think there's any value or virtue in that attitude? You have to decide; you have to weigh it out for yourself, right? You have to evaluate and put it on your own mental scales, and then you have to come up with your own answers for how hard should you work.

I teach kids and adults alike the ant philosophy—a well-known perspective of life that bears much truth.

Number one, *ants never quit.* Good philosophy! If they're headed somewhere, and something gets in their way to stop them, they find another way to get where they are determined to go. They'll climb over, they'll climb under, they'll climb around, they keep looking for another way. What a great philosophy for you as well—never quit looking for a way to get where you're supposed to go.

Number two, *ants think winter all summer*. That's another important philosophy. You can't be so disillusioned that you think only about how nice summer is when winter is sure to come. It's been said, "Don't build your house on the sand in the summer." Why is that good advice? Because although it's easy to build your house on the sand during the lazy days of summer's sand and sun, soon the fall rains and winter storms will wash away that house with no firm foundation. Ants are smart; they think winter all summer—they prepare for the storms in life that will arrive sooner than later. In the summer, you need to enjoy the warmth but also think storm, think rock—not only fun in the sun. Key philosophy.

Number three, *ants think summer all winter*. I'm sure all winter long ants say, "Winter won't last long. We'll soon be out here." What another great philosophy and attitude! The first warm day, the ants are out working. If it turns cold again, they dive back down into their nests; but next warm day, they're out working again. They can't wait to get active. Can't wait to get at it.

Regarding leadership skills: average people look forward to getting off work; successful people look forward to getting to work. That attitude is what starts to transform their lives into the doing, into the activity.

Number four and the last of the ant philosophy—*do all you possibly can*. How much will an ant gather during the summer to prepare for the winter? Answer, all he possibly can. What an incredible philosophy—the all you possibly can philosophy. How much should you do? All you possibly can do! You have to come up with a philosophy for how much you should do. We're all governed by our thinking, our evaluation, what we've decided and how we feel. Answering this big question is important: What should you do?

Mr. Shoaff gave me the best answer when I was 25 years old. He said, "Do all you can."

How many books should you read in the next six months? As many as you can fit into your schedule, because the book you miss won't help. What if someone missed reading the book, *Think and Grow Rich* by Napoleon Hill? Now the person is 40 and poor, not successful, and not happy—he missed reading the book. He lived in the country of opportunity, was a nice and sincere person, and he worked hard, but he didn't read the book because he didn't make reading a priority.

"Do all you can!"

There's no telling what treasure will not be found in your life if you miss reading the wisdom in this book and many others brimming with knowledge and insights to move you forward toward your goal.

How hard should you work? The ant philosophy tells it all.

A man says to me, "I'm making about $50,000 a year. My kids are doing okay. I pay my bills. Isn't $50,000 enough?" What would you say if a guy said that to you?

I said, "Yes, $50,000 a year is enough, if it's the best you can do."

We don't call enough an amount; we only call enough your best. If you're capable of making a half million dollars a year and you make $50,000 a year, we call you loser.

Now, it isn't the difference between $50,000 and $500,000 that's important. What's significant is *the full extent of your reach, that's what's important.* The only way to feel maximum good about yourself is to extend yourself to the full capacity of your reach, your intellectual reach and your physical reach, your potential, and your possibility to do the best you can.

What should you do? All you can. How many books should you read? As many as you can. How many skills should you learn? As many skills as possible. How many people should you touch? As many as you can. What all should you engage in? As many things as possible. Why not go to the max?

I have a good question for you. How tall will a tree grow? As tall as it can. Did you ever hear of a tree growing half as high as it could? No. Trees don't grow half, they grow fully. They drive their roots as deep as they can, stretch as high as they can, and produce every leaf they can. Trees go to the max.

You always have a choice to make.

Why would human beings settle for less than the max of their capacity? Simple answer, they have the power of choice to do so. The power of choice comes with the dignity of being human beings. We always have choices to make. Here are a few examples—to be all or to be part.

Get ready, this is a very interesting philosophical discussion. You can choose to be less than you were designed to be—or you can choose to be all you were designed to be. I'm merely suggesting that you ponder what the *all* might do for your life in the next one year, three years, or five years, if you refined your philosophy of activity and went for it all.

The difference in value is not the amount. If you do the best you can and you make $10,000 a year, we call that enough. If you do the best you can and you make a million dollars a year, we call that enough. Enough is not the difference between

$10,000 and $1 million. Enough is simply doing the best you can.

A group of psychiatrists invited me to lecture in Los Angeles. I thought that was fascinating. I never graduated from college, but they wanted to hear my story, so I went and talked to the psychiatrists. In the middle of my talk, I had the audacity to say, "Ladies and gentlemen, let me tell you what I think most messes with the mind."

They asked, "What do you think most messes with the mind?"

I said, "I think that simply doing less than you can is what messes with a person's mind. It causes all kinds of psychic damage. Simply being less than you can be, doing less than you could do, trying less than you could try, doing it with less enthusiasm than you could—I think it somehow damages the

Doing less than you can messes with your mind.

mind. It damages our self-image because here's what I discovered happens. The minute you turn this around and start extending yourself, it isn't the value you get from extending yourself that's the greatest value, it's how you feel about yourself that's the greatest value.

"Because it's not what we get that makes us valuable, it's what we become, and part of becoming is to see what all you can become, see what all you can do, see how much you can earn, how much you can share, how much you can start, how far you can reach, how far you can extend your influence. Now, that kind of commitment to philosophical thinking about attitude and about activity, we call this the potential for life change."

So far we've covered three of the five major pieces to the life puzzle: Number one is philosophy; number two is attitude; number three is activity. Number four of the five major pieces of life's puzzle is *results,* to see what we have become and accomplished.

RESULTS

Results is the name of the game. The quest of life, the key to life is to become skillful enough to accomplish rewarding endeavors. We revel in the results of our influence, productivity, activity, economic, social, personal, and spiritual goals reached.

In nature's metaphor, hard work is put in and when the fall harvest season time arrives, we reap what has come from the miracle of our hand and the seed and the soil and the seasons and the rain—the changes to cope with it all and see what we made out of what was available.

One of the most interesting ancient stories says a master had three servants and he gave them talents, or value. Philosophy determines value, and once you understand that you have value, the key is to see what you can do with it. That was the commission the master gave his three servants. He gave one, five talents; the other one, two; and the third one, one talent. His commission was, "See what you can do with these values."

Likewise, that's what your life is all about—see what you can do with your mind, see what you can do with your skills, see what you can do with your hands, see what you can do with your thinking, your possibilities, your capabilities. The key is to see what you can do with all you have, because you are aiming for the best results. The master said, "I'll be gone for a while and when I return, we'll go over the results."

According to the story, the master evidently was gone a reasonable time, which means he didn't return every five minutes and ask the servants what progress they made. The master didn't wait five years to return and ask about their progress—that was too long to ask about the progress they made in the long list of human values and experiences.

The master returned in a reasonable time and called together the three servants and asked one of life's most important questions, "How did you do during the time I was gone? What progress did you make? What results can you show me?"

He asked the servant who had five talents, and that servant said, "I turned five into ten." Do you think those two numbers have any significance? In higher learning, we say

Life expects us to make measurable progress in reasonable time.

it's very important to understand the numbers. These are key life questions. Should we be expected to double our values in a reasonable time? Answer, of course. Shouldn't we be expected to make progress?

For example, how many years do you want your child to spend in fourth grade? Would you say, "Well, they're nice kids, I guess I'd give them three or four years." No. You'd say, "I expect my child to complete fourth grade in one year." Three or four years is too much time to make such little progress.

Wouldn't it be important to ask those same questions all of our life? Yes, it is.

Those first-grade desks are built small—so they won't fit at age 21. Reasonable questions to ask yourself throughout your life, "What am I doing here right now? All this time has passed. Am I making progress? Am I where I need to be? Am I multiplying my talents?"

I think it's vital, according to the story, to go from five to ten in reasonable time. The master said in response to the first servant's numbers, "Good job, well done." To the second servant, the master said, "What happened to the talents I gave you?" That servant said, "I turned two into four." I find that a significant use of the talents. In part, life is a numbers game.

How many books should you read to be adequately prepared to debate the major life issues in the next ten years? Do you think it's important to come up with a pretty good reasonable number of books in a wide variety of subjects to be adequately prepared to debate the major life issues in the next ten years? The answer is, yes, of course.

These are valuable life lessons. This isn't just get-by stuff anymore. You can eat bread and have a pair of shoes and have a place to stay out of the rain and do okay—but this that you are reading right now is called higher learning for success and leadership and influence, skills that will serve you well for now and the future.

Numbers are important in many various aspects of life. For example, how many pounds overweight should you be at age 50? Approximately. None? Well, maybe one or two pounds. How about five? Or ten pounds? What if we approach fifteen? At twenty pounds overweight, we may turn on the red lights and sirens. You can't go beyond twenty extra pounds with any reasonable amount of safety for your health and your future.

Numbers are very important. When a reasonable time has passed, we need to say, "Let's go over the numbers one more time to make sure we aren't off track." Everything by longevity tends to drift off track, so we have to keep coming back to what we call mid-course corrections. If you're headed for the moon, the early guidance system when you first blast off doesn't serve for the whole trip, you have to make mid-course corrections. When heading for the moon, you can't miss. It's not like heading for Kansas City and you hit St. Louis instead.

Results are the ultimate endgame. When reasonable time has passed, reasonable-thinking people check the numbers. Whatever these numbers may represent in skills or learning or capacity or equities of mind.

Then the master said to the third servant, "I gave you one talent. What happened to it?" That servant said, "I still have the same talent." The story says that the master lost his cool, or something like that—which is the proper response to a lack of results. We must show that the insidious is unacceptable. We must show how empty life can be without measurable progress. We must get right on the problems and the challenges lest we yield too easily to what can leave our lives empty instead of full and leave us with pennies instead of fortune. We must have a proper response to a lack of results.

Jesus said to His disciples one day, "Does that fig tree have any figs?" That's an important life question if it's a fig tree. His disciple said, "No, sir. That tree doesn't have any figs." The story says that Jesus lost His cool, one of the few times He lost His cool. I call that a proper response to the lack of results. I guess the moral to the story is fig trees better have figs, especially when the Maker of the fig tree comes by. Results are the endgame.

Likewise, shouldn't we become emotional when we experience a lack of results? Shouldn't we become philosophically stronger, check the numbers, and take steps to increase our results?

I have taught kids how to be rich by age 40. If you live in America with banks and capital and money and churches and sermons and libraries and books and teaching and training and classes and rallies and inspiration, shouldn't you be rich by age 40?

If you're not, isn't something wrong? There's nothing wrong with the country, the community, the library and the books, and there's nothing wrong with the churches, the sermons, the school and the teachers, and there's nothing wrong with you. But, there's something wrong with your philosophy, somebody sold you the wrong plan. It's easy to buy into the wrong philosophy, and make errors in judgment that compound into pennies instead of treasure.

One of the major reasons to look at results is to see what might be wrong with activity. Maybe it's the wrong activity that's producing poor results. Many people work hard, but are not making much progress. A lesson taught in leadership skills—don't mistake movement for achievement. It's easy to get faked out by being busy. The key is not just being busy, the key is doing what needs to be done. It's easy to be busy making figure eights instead of making much progress by moving ahead straight toward your goal. Always look at results to see if there may be some difficulty with the lack of or misdirected activity.

Activity may be an area where we may need to go to work, because it takes activity to bring enterprise into being. Disciplined activity is like birthing pains. Now, I'm short on experience here, but I'm sure the mothers reading this would say giving birth ain't easy. But it wasn't meant to be easy. Everything of value is meant to be costly. The only way we can appreciate a value is by its cost. If it doesn't cost much, we probably wouldn't call it valuable.

True winning is of great worth, but the price is to play with all your heart and mind and perhaps do some losing sometimes so that when you do win, boy, the worth and the value of the winning becomes a high appreciation simply because we understand both sides of the price and promise equation.

When we look at activity and results, maybe we see that something's wrong with attitude. Maybe it's how we feel. Maybe we've been nudged off course by influence into how we think about society and how we think about taxes and government, and how we think about churches and sermons and people and schooling and learning and classes and worth and value and community and ideology. It's feelings about all that.

Then if the results aren't there, look at your philosophy. Have this conversation with yourself: "Where have I missed in the refinement of my thinking? Because my thinking has brought me here. Maybe I need some changes in my thoughts, my thinking, the books, the classes, the lessons, the studies, the decision-making, errors in judgment. If I went back and corrected some errors in judgment, would it affect the next three years?" The answer is, yes, of course. The new equity would be astounding, the new treasure would be exciting, simply by making some corrections in philosophy. Take a great deal of time to look at results, to check errors, and make corrections.

LIFESTYLE

Number five of the five pieces of life's puzzle is *lifestyle*. *Lifestyle is simply how you choose to live, how you design your life*. It's key to understand that some people have learned to *earn* well, but they haven't learned to *live* well. People study economics, but they didn't study lifestyle; so they have the money, but not the joy.

Lifestyle is figuring ways to live uniquely. It's a study, it's a practice, it's an art. It's as much of a skill as economics; learning to live well, finding ways to bring joy, pleasure, excitement, appreciation, and awareness of how unique life can be. A healthy and satisfying lifestyle doesn't come by accident. Happiness is not an accident, it's an art.

Lifestyle is not an amount. Culture is not an amount. Sophistication is not an account. Sophistication is a practice, it's an art, and anybody who wishes can engage in the art of sophistication. Understanding the difference between trinkets and treasures, lifestyle.

Lifestyle— living well.

3

THE HUMAN TOUCH OF WORDS

To take charge of your life, you must be good at communicating. In fact, you have to be aware of your everyday communication with others, thinking of it as a practice session to get better so when the real important occasions arise, you will have the gift and you'll have the style. Practice improves the sharpness, clarity, substance, and emotion.

GOOD COMMUNICATION SKILLS

Good communications is at the top of the priority list of leadership skills. Of all the skills to learn, this must be up front, major, learning by language to affect somebody else's life and mind, learning by words and phrases and sentences to effectively communicate with other people. Here's where part of the fortune lies, the use of language. There's power and authority in good communications. There's connection in the human touch of words. It was said the pen is mightier than the sword. That's true. Words are powerful.

Words translate an interchange of thought and ideas between people.

An ancient verse says, "God was the Word, and the Word was God." Strong language to illustrate how powerful the Word is. Words can be life-changing. Words can give life. Words can formulate ideologies, democracy, freedom, capitalism, and everything we enjoy in this unique country. We have to find ways to give words to all our good fortune so it can be understood. Words form the pictures of our minds. Words help to translate an interchange of thought and ideas between human beings.

One of the most important skills of good communication is to learn an abundance and variety of words, phrases, sentences, whether written or spoken. Language can powerfully affect our lives and other people's lives.

There are four steps to achieve and use good communication skills. These are basic fundamentals. Someone has said,

"Being successful is not doing extraordinary things. Success is simply doing ordinary things extraordinarily well." So let's talk about some fairly ordinary things and see if we can't find an extraordinary way to put it into action.

There are four steps to becoming a good communicator:

1. Have something good to say.

2. Say it well.

3. Read your audience.

4. Load your words with intensity.

1. HAVE SOMETHING GOOD TO SAY

Number one, have something good to say. Of course, that's an obvious first step. But remember, success is a study of the obvious, a refined study. So to achieve good communications, first of all, you have to have something to say that people want or need to hear. In computer language, it's very simple. Nothing in. Nothing out. You can't speak what you don't know. You can't share what you don't feel, and you can't translate what you don't understand. You can't give what you don't possess.

So to give it, to share it, and for what you have to say to be effective, you have to have it. All good communication starts with preparation, a keyword. *Preparation is simply getting ready.* A big share of our life is simply getting ready. The first five years of life was to get us ready to start our formal education. The next nine years prepared us for high school, which prepared us for higher education if we chose to attend college or university.

Seventeen or more years is a long time to prepare to be gainfully employed and earn a living—to get out there in the marketplace and see what we can do. A lot of life is just simply getting ready, preparation.

Now, to get ready to be a good communicator, you have to spend part of your year, part of your day getting ready for the next day, part of the week getting ready for the next week. It's so easy to be casual about not continually preparing for the next day, the next week, the next month, the next year, getting ready. Yet, communicating is one of the most important areas to be prepared. Keyword: research, continual research.

It's easy to hope that the skills that you learned in high school or college will last through your career and that the information you gathered will be sufficient for many years forward, but not so. We must continually learn, continually grow. Preparation is building an account from which you can draw what you need when you need it to communicate effectively with a variety of people. When you get ready to talk, make sure you have a verbal check that you can cash.

The power of good communication is obvious when what you say is only the tip of the iceberg of all you know. When you are prepared and ready for the moment, this time, this occasion, what you say will be impactful, interesting, and will hold the listener's attention.

I'm sure you've been around people who have told you more than they knew. And it didn't take them but a short period of time to run out of illustrations, to exhaust all their

Prepare on purpose!

stories, meaning they were not prepared to communicate effectively.

Now I must admit it is possible in some respects to go through life learning by accident. There are some things you can learn by just careening from wall to wall and stumbling from day to day and staggering from week to week. But the other 99 percent of what you need to know has to be on purpose. *Preparation on purpose*—good phrase.

Ask yourself, "Am I engaged in preparation on purpose to get me ready to use the communication skills necessary to take me where I want to go?" Good question. Do you have a good answer?

That's why you're reading this book, to ask yourself some of the tough questions. And being able to answer them.

When I met Mr. Shoaff, he asked me the tough questions. I was 25 years old. He said, "Mr. Rohn, you've been working six years." I started working when I was 19. Then he asked me a simple question, "Mr. Rohn, how are you doing?"

I said, "Not very well."

Mr. Shoaff said, "I suggest you not do that anymore."

Another question, "Mr. Rohn, how much money have you invested in the last six years?"

"Not any."

Shoaff said, "Who sold you on that plan?"

Wow, tough questions. It's so important for somebody to come along and ask us the tough questions and not let us get by with small numbers and small answers.

So that's what I'm doing for you in this book, asking some of the tough questions.

KEY COMMUNICATION WORDS

Key words to prepare you for exhibiting good communications and being a good communicator: interest; fascination; sensitivity; knowledge. Let's look at each in more detail.

Interest

Number one, *interest*. To prepare for communicating in the best way possible, I urge you to take a new interest in life. Here's a good pledge to make at the beginning of the day, "I'm going to be more interested in this day. I'm going to see if I can get more from the day."

It's easy to just try to get *through* the day. But sophisticated, successful people learn to get *from* the day. They don't want a day to go by without gathering up new ideas, new impressions, new color, new nuances, new sense of worth and value. They gather from the day, interest. Two of the major subjects to *study with interest are life and people.* Develop a new, sharper interest and focus on life and people, what's happening, what's going on.

Your new commitment to a new interest for the day gets you ready for the years to come because with interesting topics to talk about comes new opportunities to share with others. You will be able to say it well because you know what you're talking about, because you went through the laborious process of gathering, extracting, and processing the information for your benefit and the future benefit of others who will reap the wisdom you have to share. So the first key word is interest.

Two major subjects to study with interest— life and people.

Fascination

Here's the second word, *fascination,* which is a bit beyond just simple interest. Interested people are satisfied that it ticks, and that's good to know. But fascinated people want to know what makes it tick. Fascinated people aren't satisfied, usually, with surface information. They have to know more than just what appears. They want to know what's really going on.

Back in the 1960s, the hippies were often heard asking, "What's happening?" Good question. "Sophisticated" hippies may have asked, "What's *really* happening?" As in what's really going on? What's making things happen? Why do people feel what they feel and think like they think? What is the difference between success and failure? Who has the appetite, and who doesn't have the appetite to do better in life?

I urge you to absorb a whole new fascination about life and people and circumstances and society and money and banks and churches and sermons and books and records and life experiences and enterprise and nations and color and races and religion—an exciting fascination for the entire wide and wonderful panorama of life and life experiences. If you take a sincerely fascinated look at what's going on at home, work, in the community, and beyond, your perspective will expand and show up in living color and obvious sharpness in future communications with everyone you meet. Your conversations will have a new reach and a new depth—new insight and new excitement.

To test that theory of mine, I have a good experiment for you to try. The next time you're tempted to be frustrated, see if you can turn that situation into fascination. Turning frustration into fascination is an excellent skill to learn. My example: I'm sitting on the freeway in Los Angeles. My airplane leaves in 45 minutes. The traffic is not moving an inch. Can I turn this frustrating experience into something fascinating? Yes! I can concentrate on the weather or think about what people in the cars around me are having—some of whom may be facing direr circumstances than just missing a plane. Maybe a parent is thankful for the extra time to spend with the children in the car after a busy morning. Try to turn frustration into fascination.

If a smile comes across your face, other people will wonder what's going on and will probably smile too. But it'll just be private between you and me—you'll remember reading this trick when taking charge of your life in frustrating situations. Turning frustration into fascination is an essential discipline and skill to learn.

Sensitivity

The next significant keyword is *sensitivity*. To really communicate well and connect with people in a variety of ways, you have to have felt the experience for yourself. It has to be part of you. Sensitivity training means being touched, or affected, by a wide range of human experience, perhaps even beyond your own.

Incredible words have been written about the master teacher, Jesus. It's said He was "moved" with compassion. What was happening moved Him. It touched Him. He was affected. And on more than one occasion, He cried. So in my mind, part of the human drama of experience, is for us to really be able to reach people and touch people with words and ideas and emotion and phrases and sentences loaded with feelings; therefore, we have to be aware of this area of sensitivity, which is being touched, being affected by our own life experiences as well as the lives of other people.

Sensitivity—being touched, being moved—is part of the heavyweight stuff that will show up in our language and in our communication. I've lived a rather sheltered life, so I've had to really work on this. What do I know about tragedy? I've never had any tragedy. But part of the world is tragic. Part of life is tragic. If you don't at least try to understand the dark side of life, the tragic side, the extreme sorrow side, your life is left a bit shallow.

Sometimes when you live a sheltered life, you have to, at times, venture outside of your own small world of secluded experiences and see for yourself what it is like to live as someone else might have lived, if possible. At least try to be touched by the experiences of others. You can't really know till you live it. I understand that. But at least you can try to put yourself in another person's shoes, so to speak. If you do your homework here in sensitivity to gain a wider range of experience than your own, I promise that extra worth will show up in your conversation and in your communication—revealing a deeper and more compassionate you.

When I lived in northern California, I used to go to San Francisco two or three times a year to spend a day in the Tenderloin. For a farm boy from Idaho, the Tenderloin area in San Francisco, was quite an experience. I saw what we call the other side. I always came away with a whole new sense of the great distance between failure and success, the whole distance between goodness and evil, between despair and joy.

When you take the opportunity to walk through a lifestyle different from your own, you come away with more of a sense of value because the true values of life come by the contrast.

Unless you experience more of the contrast, even the values you consider valuable become a bit shallow, if you don't understand the contrast.

It's hard to really appreciate winning until you've done some losing. It's hard to appreciate success until you've done some failing. If you've done some failing, success now becomes a much larger worth and value and commodity, when you understand a bit of the other side.

So part of acquiring sensitivity is to deliberately go. Where? Wherever there are experiences beyond your own to get somewhat of an education as to the contrast of life and the differences. You will educate your mind and educate your spirit. Sure enough, that extra worth will start showing up in your sentences and your words, which will become weightier, heavier. They'll mean more when you talk to somebody.

I met Frank, the bartender in a sleazy little bar in the Tenderloin. Frank sees more tragedy in a week than most people see in a lifetime. One day I was visiting Frank and we were talking. Frank asked, "See that lady sitting over there on the barstool?"

And I said, "Yes."

"How old do you think she is?"

I said, "She's 45."

Frank said, "She's 25."

Wow, I thought.

He said, "That's Cookie. Cookie used to be a go-go dancer back in the go-go days. She developed some kind of bone disease in her legs and her hips. Now she's had all kinds of operations with the bolts and the pins trying to hold her together. Now she's a cripple and can hardly walk. So her go-go days are over."

Sure enough, I could see that Cookie was severely crippled.

Frank says, "Cookie also has a little boy, five years old, and he's dying of leukemia. Cookie comes several times a week, sits on that barstool and plays a little music to try to cheer up her life. She usually drinks far too much and gets wasted, and I have to call a taxi to come and take her home."

Wow, I thought, *How come her life worked out like that and my life worked out like this? How come I get to travel around the world and Cookie finds it hard to even get home?*

That kind of exposure, that kind of sensitivity, that kind of study of another human being. I know you can't really know someone else's entire life story unless we lived it. I understand that. But you can go a great deal into trying to understand a wider range of human experience. And if you allow those experiences touch you, let them affect you, let them educate you, let them give you a broader range of emotional wealth and worth, I'm telling you that extra worth will start showing up in your language, your words, and in your presence.

You can touch people you couldn't touch before. You can reach people you couldn't reach before you had the experience. Your words will draw people in more than they did before, just by going through some of these encounters.

So I'm asking you to consider the word *sensitivity,* and ask yourself, "What can I engage in to give me a broader range of understanding human suffering as well as human joy, of the dilemma as well as the confidence, of the joy as well as the sorrow, of the success as well as the failures of life?"

I strongly encourage you to gain an understanding in a broader sense and let that have an effect on your future ability to touch and reach others. Keyword, sensitivity.

Knowledge

Good communication starts with this laborious task of gathering *(working) knowledge*. Working knowledge is knowledge that you deliberately gather that will work for you in the future. This is why Mr. Shoaff taught me to keep journals.

He said, "Gather working knowledge, knowledge that you go back over, knowledge that you review, ideas that you go back through one more time to find the extra meaning, the extra depth, the extra worth, the extra value, working knowledge."

Your library, the books you read, the deliberate attempts to broaden your understanding, these disciplines are very important in bettering your communication skills—ever-increasing amounts of the refinement of intellect. Working knowledge.

HAVE SOMETHING GOOD TO SAY

We covered interest, fascination, sensitivity, and knowledge, which all support my number-one point in good communications—have something good to say.

I was asked to give a talk to a service club and was trying to think of a good topic for my noon lecture. I came up with, "The four ifs that make life worthwhile." I thought that was something good to say—and to write here for you.

First, life is worthwhile, if you learn. Your own experiences can be a great teacher. Over the past three years, you've probably been doing life right, or doing it wrong. Mr. Shoaff pointed that out to me when I was 25. He said, "Don't ignore the last six years. Six years is a pretty good chunk of time to go over and evaluate and put on the scales and say, 'It either weighs or it doesn't weigh.' You're either on track or off track." I offer you the same advice, take a look at your own past experiences—have you been learning?

Another way to learn is from other people's experiences. Gather up someone else's experiences, other people's experiences (OPE). If somebody went through a tragic or exciting experience for five years and the person wrote a book you could read in five days, wouldn't that be an exceptional advantage? Yes—if you read the book. This is not casual stuff I'm telling you. This is the extraordinary kind of learning and skills that's necessary, I think, to gain the high life treasures.

I think the time and effort and discipline is a small price to pay for lifelong treasures—the extra reading, the extra commitment to the excellence of learning. Life is worthwhile, if you learn.

Second, life is worthwhile, if you try. You have to try with what you know. Can you win the next game? Make the next sale? Write the next great novel? Enjoy the next class? You don't know—unless you try. Commit yourself to try.

When the final book on you is written, let it show your wins and let it show your losses, but don't let it show you didn't play. How would you explain that? So you have to play. You have to try. See what you can do with your life. See what you can do with the next game. The key to life is to give it a try.

I put the bar up three feet and ask the kids, "Who can jump three feet?" I get a whole variety of responses. "I don't think so." "I'm not sure." "I don't know." "Yes, I can." I say, "Well, how are we going to know? You have to take a run at it." I don't know any other way. You just have to take a run at it.

Likewise, who knows if you can jump three feet till you try? If you try and knock the bar down, does that mean you can't jump three feet? No. So try it again. Try it over. Try it another time. Try it another way. Try it with more speed. There's all kinds of ways to try. Many challenges will come your way— don't give up, try and try again until you overcome each one.

Third, life is worthwhile, if you stay. You have to learn to hang in there. You must learn to stay from spring till fall. Many people plant in the spring and leave in the summer. They're gone the first hot day.

I thought for sure John would last a month. I asked, "Where's John?"

"I don't know, somebody said, 'Boo,' and he quit."

To win, you have to learn to stay. Just because you're behind in the first quarter, don't leave. You have to stay and hang in there. A person in charge of his life builds a foundation and then he stays to build on that foundation, adding walls and a roof. He doesn't walk off, wander away and build another foundation. Hang in there for the long haul—there's strength to gain in staying.

Fourth, life is worthwhile, if you care. Caring is an important human value. I wrote, "If you care at all, you'll get *some* results. If you care enough, you'll get *incredible* results." Caring—to care for the day and to use its time; to care for the people and to help them with their possibilities; to care for the enterprise, its dignity and its reputation; and to care for yourself to become all you can become, stretch as far as you can stretch, accomplish as much as you can accomplish, become all that you can become.

Caring is having something good to say. The first step to good communications is preparation—research, getting ready, making deposits in your mental, spiritual, moral bank account upon which to draw.

2. SAY IT WELL

The second step to achieve good communications is to say what you have to say well. We have finally gotten to it. When you have something good to say, number two is obvious, learn to say it well. Once you have the information and the awareness and the understanding, the knowledge, now the key to good communication is how to translate it into meaningful words, emotions, feelings, phrases, sentences, paragraphs. It's very important to be able to translate it so the listener can benefit from what you're saying.

Learning to say it well is a whole subject worth a weekend of study. Let me just give you a short list of suggestions on learning to say it well:

- Repetition
- Brevity
- Style
- Vocabulary

Number one, **repetition.** It takes practice to say it well. I don't know any substitute for practice. To learn any skill, you just have to go through it again and again and again. My first attempt at lecturing, especially outside my own comfortable business circles, was pretty tough.

Learning to say it well was a struggle for me. But I kept at it and kept at it, and now I'm better. One of my seminars is titled "Challenge to Succeed." It's about four hours long, and I can do it without any notes. Every once in a while, someone asks me, "You lectured this evening for four hours without any notes. How can you do that?"

I say, "It's very simple. I've done it a few thousand times." That's simplicity. You just do it over and over and often.

I have another good question for you, "How long do you want it to take to get good at what you do?" You probably respond by saying, "Not very long." Then you have to do it often. Repetition starts the skill. Repetition must be done with the objective of getting better. Sometimes it's easy to be casual about repetition, which means you won't get much better. How about the man who's been making presentations for ten years, and he's made the same verbal errors for ten years!

Perhaps ten years ago, he said, "I don't quite know how to put this." And ten years later, he's saying, "I don't quite know how to put this."

Listeners say, "Hey, ten years is too long not to know how to put it. We can give you ten hours not to know how to put it. You can stretch our patience and take ten days not to know how to put it, but we can't give you ten years!" Ten years is too long not to make enough progress in better language skills.

Repetition with purpose is vital. The purpose of repetition is to grow and to change, to develop, to expand, to make progress—to make improvements on a well-crafted, well-said commentary, sales pitch, presentation, whatever needs to be said.

Saying it well also includes sincerity—speaking from the heart with noble intent, intending to bring value. Sincerity adds immeasurably to your ability to speak well and communicate effectively. There's no substitute for sincerity. I can forgive you for a mistake in judgment, but I can't forgive you for a mistake in intent.

Number two: **brevity.** Part of saying it well is to be brief. Don't linger too long on one subject when speaking. I've discovered in my lecturing and speaking around the world that I can't linger too long on any one point because the listeners lose interest.

I used to tell stories that were too long, I went on and on. By the time I hit the punchline, people forgot how it started—and the punchline didn't make sense. Too long. Brevity is very important because the human attention span is short. You have only a short amount of time to say what you have to say before you lose your audience.

Jesus, the master communicator, was probably the best in selecting His team. He looked at someone and said, "Follow me." That's brief. That's short. He was brief and yet effective. Of course, because of who He was, He didn't have to say more.

I think sometimes we try to make up in words what we lack in self-confidence. So part of the key to being brief is personal development, personal growth, personal awareness, understanding self-worth. Being self-confident allows you can use the economy of words. This is a good position to be in—what you are adds so much weight to what you say that you don't have to say very much to get your point across. Brevity is a good point when saying it well.

Number three: **style.** There are many aspects of style, from body language and gestures to facial expressions and eyes and emotion. Style plays a very important role in communication.

Communicating well is not just about the subject matter—it's also about your delivery style. Style is important to attract attention, to emphasize a point, to provoke a response. A couple of helpful points on style: Be a student of style, don't copy someone's style. Make sure that the style study becomes distinctly you. Also be a student of how someone speaks—tone, pace, etc.—perhaps borrow bits and pieces from people you admire and the way they can communicate.

Then make sure that all of your research and study blends into your own distinctive style. There is a wide variety of styles and yours will become apparent the longer you practice and learn to feel what seems to fit best.

John the Baptist had a unique style. He came out of the desert dressed in camel's hair, and his diet was grasshoppers and wild honey. He screamed and yelled and thundered curses on the king and other people. That was his style. People came to see John, I'm sure. I'm sure the word was out. "You have to come and see this guy." Not just what he said, but his style, I'm sure, was something to watch. John had a unique style that attracted people to him to hear what he had to say. His cousin, Jesus, had a whole different style, His own unique style—and multitudes were attracted to Him as well.

As you study your own style, don't be afraid to ask, "How is my style coming across? Should I emphasize more? Should

I learn to be more emphatic? How is my tone of voice?" All these details and many more concern style.

Four is **vocabulary.** Saying it well means using the proper choice of words. To build my early vocabulary, I used to write on a card three or four words and definitions and put it on my car's sun visor. Back in those days, I traveled a lot by car.

Sure enough, by the end of the day I had expanded my vocabulary. Some of my friends took a survey among prisoners in New England and made a very important discovery for a rehabilitation program they were working on. They discovered that there is definitely a relationship between vocabulary and behavior. The more limited the vocabulary, the more tendency toward poor behavior. I found it amazing that vocabulary would affected behavior.

Thinking about it for a while, it makes sense. Here's why. Vocabulary is a way of seeing. One reason for vocabulary is to interpret what we see, to interpret what we hear. The vocabulary of the mind grapples with the words and the images that come to our mind. So if you have a limited or poor set of words and skills and tools with which to interpret, you can imagine the errors and the mistakes you make in judgment. Since vocabulary is a way of seeing, if you can't see well, you can imagine the errors and how they compound as life unfolds.

With vocabulary we interpret and we express. The words we know are the only words available to us. The words we know are the only tools available to us to interpret what's going on, to interpret what's being said, and to express your heart and your mind. If you can't interpret well and if you can't express well, you can imagine what a deterrent that is to the good life and the extra treasures, feelings, awareness, riches, power, and influence. So it's very wise to have a good, large vocabulary.

One of the most valuable books in your library should be a dictionary. I urge you to go through the dictionary every now and then. Words are fascinating, their origin and meanings.

Don't forget to say it—is the last part of *say it well*. Practice the art of saying well what you have to say. Every chance you get, say it well. It's easy to be lazy in language and not practice the gift and the art.

Then when it comes time to make an important talk, to appeal to a child, to chat with a coworker, to convince a customer, if we don't practice the skills of good communication, it will become a habit to come across as mediocre rather than exceptional.

Actions are no substitute for words.

We can quickly forget words, drop the sharpness and clarity, and hesitate to use the vocabulary we know simply because we don't practice every day. If you want to be a good communicator, and improve how you communicate, you have to be aware of how you are speaking each time you open your mouth. Then when the real important occasions arise, you will have the gift and you'll have the style. You'll have the sharpness and the clarity and the substance and the emotion. Speaking with confidence will become natural and easy.

Remember this key phrase—actions are no substitute for words. Don't fail to say it. You may have heard the old expression, words are no substitute for action. That's true. Talk, talk, talk, and never act is not good. But act, act, act, and never talk is not good either. We must be gifted with words if we want the full treasure of life. So practice on every occasion.

For example, it's nice to send somebody flowers, but flowers have a limited vocabulary. About the best flowers can say is you remembered or you care, that's about all. Flowers can't say, "You are an incredible part of my life. Nobody in this world affects me like you do." Along with the flowers, write on the card something from your heart. Add the gift of words to work with the action.

You will start to sense a whole growing excitement about using language to affect somebody, to translate feelings of heart and mind. The response and results you receive will grow immensely. I'm asking you to take extra time to engage in these arts and practices—the gift of language, communications, affecting people with words.

3. READ YOUR AUDIENCE

So we've covered the first two steps to good communications: have something good to say; say it well. Step three is *read your audience*. To read and to pick up the signals of what's happening with your audience is a necessary skill. When I first started lecturing outside my business circles, I had some problems reading my audience.

My early audiences could have left halfway through my lecture—and I'd have never known it. I was so intent on what I was saying that I was a bit unconscious of what was going on out there. Then I finally learned to look up, to watch and see the people who were listening to me—I learned how to read the audience, an integral part of speaking.

My largest audience has been 10,000. I wasn't the only speaker; others included Art Linkletter, Paul Harvey, Dr. Peele, and Zig Ziglar. We each had an hour. This was the first time I'd ever talked to 10,000 people. Awesome event for me.

Paul Harvey didn't have any problem. Art Linkletter didn't have any problem. But I had some problems for the first four or five minutes. Reading 10,000 people takes time and that many people can turn on a speaker quickly. So if you want to be effective, you have to get feedback. You have to pick up the signals to know whether to be stronger or to ease off, whether to change stories, change words, change language.

All of this comes from perfecting a good ability to read your audience. So let me give you some clues on reading:

1. **Listen.** Part of reading is simply listening. You pick up a lot of clues as to what else to say, what all to say, by being a good listener. From early times, I think we've learned to be somewhat good speakers, but we have to be good listeners

as well. That's where you pick up the information, by listening well, especially in a private conversation, more informal conversations. Good listening habits are part of reading an audience, crowd, or gathering.

2. **Read what you see.** There's a good book titled *How to Read a Person Like a Book* by Gerard Nierenberg and Henry Calero. It's a study of body language. I caution you not to get too deeply involved in this and become so intent on reading body language that you may miss the point. But we can all, I think, use help in this area. Some things are very obvious. For example, you're talking to somebody and he has his arms folded, his chin is tucked down, and he's frowning. That probably means you have your work cut out for you. You need to reach deep into your bag of experiences and language because this person isn't going to be easy to connect with.

So some body language is fairly obvious. If you're talking to somebody and she leans toward the door, that probably means that you're not going to have her as an audience much longer. Part of reading a person is just being conscious of body language, reading what you see.

Kids are pretty easy to read because they don't even try to fake you out. If you're boring them, they just stare out the window. They don't mind showing you their total unconcern.

But what's more challenging is that in polite society, sometimes body language can be deceiving. If somebody, while you're talking, looks at you and smiles, make sure you don't misread that. We teach in leadership skills not to mistake courtesy or kindness for consent and acceptance. In polite society, we learn to be courteous, but that doesn't mean we buy the story. If someone is being polite, smiling, and nodding, don't misread that and stop short of the full persuasion.

3. **Reading the emotional signals** is probably the most effective but the most elusive. This is an area where women have more expertise than men—picking up emotional signals. I think men can learn these skills, but I think women have a lot of this instinctively. All good communicators have to learn how to pick up emotional signals, noticing whether or not to change our language, be sharper or softer, to go after a problem or ease back and give it time to soak in. Part of this is just picking up on the feelings, the emotions, being sensitive to the situation. This is not easy stuff. This is extra learning stuff, extra skills. This is called summit learning, the extra measures of rewards that come from communicating by learning these extra skills. So third, very important to read your audience. How are you coming across? What is the effect? From a child to an auditorium full of people, reading, reading.

4. **Load your words with intensity.** We discussed three steps to good communication: have something good to say; say it well; and read your audience. Number four is load your words with intensity. Here starts the power of what we say. Part of the strength of what we say is the words we choose. The greater part of the strength of what we say is the emotions loaded into the words. Words loaded with emotion have power unmatched. In fact, there is no greater power.

Words have an effect, but words loaded with emotion have an incredible effect. My words may reach you, but if I can't touch you with my spirit, if I can't touch you with my emotions, my feelings, my beliefs, then I probably haven't affected you very much. We might describe words like a straight pin. Sometimes when guys buy a folded dress shirt, there are numerous little pins in it. If I took one of those little straight pins, threw it at you, and it hit you in the face or the hand, you'd probably feel it. That means I got you with my words.

There is great power in words loaded with emotion.

But what if I took that straight pin and wired it to the end of an iron bar and then hit you with it? I had the power to drive that pin through your heart. The reason? The pin is the words, but the iron bar is the emotion, the feeling, the belief, the commitment, all that I am. If I can put more of what I am into what I say, no telling what miracle I can produce, no telling how much of an effect I can be. Real persuasion comes from putting *you* into what you say.

Now for an extra refinement of leadership skills lesson— learning to measure your emotions. We must learn how to measure our emotions. For example, we don't shoot a cannon at a rabbit. It's effective, but the rabbit is obliterated. There is too much firepower for the occasion. You don't need an atomic explosion to make a minor point. Enough, but not too much. This is understanding how to measure the flow of our emotions to cover a point.

But if the point you want to make needs heavyweight stuff, you reach and get it, because you have the vocabulary you need and you have read your audience. If it needs a milder approach, you learn how to measure it in milder, easier terms. So, it's very important to measure your emotions, your feelings.

What do I mean by intensity and emotions? All of your experiences and how they have affected you, that's the sum total of your emotional content, where you've been and what you've heard and what you've seen and who you've met and this whole panorama of life experiences for you up until now and how you felt about all that—that we call the sum total of your emotions.

Consequently, the key is to learn how to measure all that and put effective amounts into the words you choose. The key to effective communications—well-chosen words loaded with well-measured emotions.

In the gift of an actor's performance, the splendid performance comes from knowing with skill how to use language and how to use emotions. When the time calls for it, emotions kept close to the surface put into well-chosen words can make the most dramatic effect on someone's mind and heart. You can't believe the extent of your reach when you engage in these communication skills. You have the power to not only take charge of your own life, but to make a positive impact on other people's lives as well.

4

CONNECTIONS

To really make a difference in your life, you need to know how to effectively make a difference in other people's lives. To do that, start with where they are before you try to take them to where you want them to go. Meet people where they are. If somebody's hurting, you have to meet in the hurt. If somebody's in trouble, you have to start with the trouble.

Four essential components in making connections—with yourself and other people—are explained in this chapter: 1) identification; 2) logic and reason; 3) attack problems; 4) solutions.

IDENTIFICATION

Another piece to the communication connection challenge is to identify with people. Now it's not too difficult to identify with someone if he or she is like you. The real challenge is to identify with somebody who's *not* like you. In a wider range of this teaching, the reaction you want from identification is, "Me too!" You want someone's reaction to be, "Me too. I understand what that's like. I've been there." So part of translating your experiences into words is to connect with people so they identify with you.

Here's the reaction you don't want, "So what?" If you're not careful to load your presentation with emotion, you may get a lot of, "So whats."

Mr. Shoaff, who only went to the eighth grade in school, was very wise nonetheless. He gave me a classic point to ponder when I was 25 years old. It was put in such simple terms, yet I've never forgotten it. He said, "Learn to express not impress." That advice was so helpful, because it's so easy to engage in language designed to impress instead of express. But Shoaff said, "If you want to touch people's hearts and minds, learn to express." Sincerity from the heart, not impress from the ego.

"Learn to express not impress."

Impress builds a gulf, express builds a bridge. Identification is a whole wide subject in itself. The identification question we're asking in the book's context is what makes me real to my audience? What makes me real to a child, a teen, an adult? Identification builds a bridge. When meeting someone for the first time, you're simply getting acquainted, building a bridge, making contact. Find something you have in common. That's where you start, something you have in common.

When we have seminars at our ranch at Clear Lake, everybody easily gets acquainted—because almost everybody gets lost trying to find the ranch. Ha! Right? What a great way to start conversations. "Did you get as lost as I did trying to find this place?" Somebody says, "Yeah, was that you up there taking the wrong turn? I thought that was you." What a great way to get acquainted. Most people have had a similar experience, like getting lost, so try and find something you both have in common, no matter how small or seemingly trivial.

One of the greatest communicators of all time is Paul, an apostle of early Christian history. He didn't have any problem talking to sinners, because he claimed to be a chief sinner. Wow, what an identification point. Do you think sinners would listen to a chief sinner? Of course. He identified with them, and them with him. What a way to begin, right?

The key is to start where the person or audience is. If they need help in your area of expertise, so much the better—you are immediately in a position to help and can identify with the person. If you meet someone who just needs an ear to listen or a shoulder to cry on, no doubt he or she will say something that you can identify with, and the connection is made.

COMMONALITY

When you meet somebody and you try to help, listen first and then your conversation will have substance, meaning, and depth after you find something in common. Then you start there to build a bridge and the path toward solving the problem. Identification.

If you work in any way with children, the next section may be of special interest. Children, after all, are our future and instilling pertinent and stabilizing disciplines at an early age will set the stage for a lifetime.

So how do you identify with a child? It's tough. What if you're 40 and the child is 12? That a long bridge to build. It isn't always easy. In fact, we used to call it the generation gap. So how do you manage the skills that build the bridge between the generation gap? There are answers.

First, it helps to remember when you were 12. Take time to go back and remember what life looked like when you were 12 years old. This is similar to what an actor does when digging into a character role. They go back in their memory and relive the joys and adventures, hurts and emotions, fun and excitement, the trauma and the drama of the sum total of their life back in the early years. Likewise, go back through all that and let it affect you one more time. Let it wash over you one more time. Let it rekindle one more time. You say, "Well, it may be painful." That's true, but you have go back through those experiences to reach people, of any age, who are in pain.

I don't have any problem working with 12-year-olds, because I remember almost every day of being 12. Age 12 is a fascinating year. I remember quite well that one of the challenges of being 12, is you're not 13. If I heard it once, I heard it a hundred

Identify on a personal level.

times when I was 12, "You're only 12," as if that was some awful place to be, right? The teenagers would say, "Of course, you can't go, you're only 12." I always had the same thought, *Wow, I can't wait to be rid of 12 and become a teenager.* So, pretty frustrating. If you want to reach somebody 12, go back and remember being 12—identify on a personal level.

Were you ever chosen last when you were a kid? The scene goes something like this. They're choosing up sides to play a game:

"I'll take you."

"I'll take you."

"I'll take you."

Then you're the only one who hasn't be picked, and you're standing there by yourself, and the next leader says, "Well, I guess I'll have to take you."

Wow, what a humiliating experience. But go back and relive it, let it smite you one more time. Let it hit you and hurt you. Because to really affect people, you have to be moved and you have to be touched. Without the moving and touching of life experiences, whatever emotion it calls for, there are some people you can't reach unless you can share in their pain.

Another key way to reach people is to read all the books they are reading or have read. This is called doing your homework. Lack of homework shows in the marketplace. Lack of homework shows at home. One of the greatest places we can meet someone is in discussing a book. I say, "Remember the story where...?" Or "Wasn't that awesome when...?" Right away, they are excited to share other parts of the book with you. When you do your homework, it makes all the difference in how easy it is to connect.

For children, when I say, "Remember the story where...?" and they respond knowing the story, then I say, "Well, that's about like now. Not exactly, but it's pretty close." And the child says, "Oh, I see, I see!" Now they can see, because we went back to something we had in common—a book. But if you don't read the book and don't do your homework, you will miss a chance to identify with someone who needs your help and understanding.

BUILDING BRIDGES

Here's the big challenge, identifying with somebody who's not like you in color or religion or circumstance. How do successful people reach and touch and connect with people who aren't as successful? Well, first of all, they have to talk about their struggles, not their success. The key to good identification is to know that people will identify with your struggle more often than your success. If you have an hour to talk and you spend 59 minutes on your success story, you will be building a gulf, not a bridge.

Spend most of the time on your struggles, most of the time on your fears, most of the time on your apprehensions, most of the time you hesitated, most of the time you were about to give it up. Spend time telling people how you overcame all the challenges. That's called identifying and building bridges.

Then take them by the hand and show them your success when it has meaning, because it came from struggles, it came from decisions, and it came maybe from heartbreak, and it came maybe even from the same position they find themselves. Identification is what makes you real. That's so important.

Another part of identification is proper word choice. Jesus said to His disciples one day, "Today, I'm going to teach you how to fish." What an important choice of words, fish. Who is He talking to? Fishermen. That's brilliant. He didn't say, "I'm going to teach you how to recruit." No, what do they know about recruit? These fishermen don't know anything about recruit. If you insist on saying recruit to fishermen, you are naïve and your effort doomed. You have to change your vocabulary to identify with your audience to reap a harvest. In essence Jesus said, "I want to teach you how to become fishermen." Now see, they understood that language. He meant that recruiting people is a lot like fishing. They understood that—if it's like fishing, we can figure it out.

FAMILIAR LANGUAGE

Another tip to successful identification is to not use "inside lingo" on the outside world. Sometimes little catchy phrases become comfortable, but outside of your home or workplace environment, they are unfamiliar and strange.

For example, a man said to me, "We have to get into the word. We have to spend more time in the word." I thought, *How small would I have to be to get into a word?* I found out later he meant we should read the Bible more. You have to learn to shift language gears according to whom you are speaking.

A lady said to me, "I've learned how to handle my space. How are you doing with your space?" I thought, *Space, space? What's my space?* I found out later she'd been to personal space seminars and she learned spacey language. So you have to be careful not to use uncommon language that will confuse people. Only people who had attended that specific seminar would understand the spacey language.

We have to shift gears into appropriate word choices depending on our audience. It's called the gift of language in a variety of awareness to learn how to choose the right words and the right phrases, depending with whom you're talking. Be aware and perceptively sharp when you are communicating with others and you will choose the words that make sense.

You have to identify with the sorrow by recalling your own sorrow. Identify with the joy by recalling your own joy. Identify with the difficulty by rehearsing your own difficulty. Here's one of the best clues in learning to better identify.

As mentioned previously, go back over your own life and study your circumstances, your feelings, your awareness, some of the stories you haven't told for a long time, some of the experiences you've had. Sometimes when you freshly come from an experience, it isn't that easy to translate it and it isn't that easy to talk about it. But as the time passes and you can take a more thoughtful approach to your experiences, a story will emerge that others will identify with and you will build a bridge.

The key is not to lose the intensity of your life, but to become more educated in using the intensity of your experiences to weave into the next conversation, and by the gift of language and emotion, touch someone's life, reach someone, affect someone, persuade someone. Identification is a very important subject.

LOGIC AND REASON

The next part of a good presentation is logic and reason. If you're trying to persuade a child or talk to an adult, customer, or audience, part of any presentation is the logical part, the facts and the figures, and the numbers and the dimensions. I won't linger too long on this topic because here's my point on logic and reason, it has to be brief. We need some facts, but only enough facts to start the decision-making process. Beware not to cover too many facts.

You may have heard the expression, "It's possible to talk somebody into buying. But keep on talking, and you talk them out of buying." Here's where this problem usually occurs, you can talk someone into deciding, but then you keep on talking,

talking, talking and then they undecide. We talk past the objective with too much logic, too much reason. We need to talk about enough logic and reason so that it starts to make sense, not so the person understands it all.

For example, if you walk into a new car showroom and express an interest in an automobile, the salesman comes along and says, "Let me tell you about this car."

You say, "Okay."

He says, "Follow me." And he takes you back into the maintenance area, and opens the vehicle's manual and says, "Let's start with the left front wheel."

Right away you would say, "Hold it, hold it."

He says, "This is going to take a long time. There are a thousand facts here to go through."

You'd say, "Hold it, hold it. I don't need a thousand facts to decide about this automobile."

How many facts do you need? About a half dozen. And if somebody makes the mistake of going beyond the half dozen, they will lose their audience.

So make sure you don't get into a too-wide range of facts and logic. Why? Because most decisions are made emotionally. We need just enough logic so that it makes sense, but we're probably going to do it more out of an emotional desire. So the key is to be brief with logic, reasons, and facts, because too much of anything is too much at one time.

For example, what if you sat down to a steak dinner and you were real hungry, so you cleaned your plate? What if they cleared that away and brought you another steak dinner? Well, let's say you're *real* hungry, so you dig into the second one and eat it all. What if they cleared that away and brought

Brevity is key regarding logic and reason.

you a third dinner? That third plateful of food doesn't look as good as the first. It's just too much. So remember that brevity is best when it comes to logic and reason. It needs to be powerful, it needs to be factual, but brief.

ATTACK THE PROBLEMS

When taking charge of your life, learning to attack, to mount a precise attack on problems is one of the best ways to help yourself and others. The refinement of that skill that leaders must know is how to attack the problem—but not the person. This tactic is called attack and confess. One of the best ways to wage an attack is to confess you have or have had the problem.

Use yourself as example one, then use third parties. For example, say, "Let me tell you about someone I know, I'll call her Mary. If Mary was here, she would confess, but she isn't here, so I'll confess for her. Mary put off dealing with her problem and it got worse and worse until she became.... If she was here, she would probably try to persuade you with tears because the problem became so intense." We call that using a third party to address a problem.

So what problems are you facing that need to be attacked and destroyed? Let me give you some common examples that affect many people: procrastination; contempt versus compassion; blame; excuses. There is a long list of problems that people encounter. Here I include only four of most prevalent problems—you can continue this study on your own.

PROCRASTINATION

Procrastination is front and center. You have to attack procrastination, because it's so insidious. It eats up such large chunks of your life and leaves you in a small corner of what can be a large and wonderful life. Putting off, delaying, letting things slide are the obvious tactics of a procrastinator.

I'm one of the best people to know how to attack procrastination, because I have confessed to being one of the all-time great procrastinators. I've done a lot in my lifetime, but I've also put a lot of things off. I am so good at procrastination, I could teach it. I can show you how to procrastinate so that no one ever knows you're doing it, so that it doesn't show. I mean, I'm really good at it.

But I also know the pain of procrastination. I also know the regret that comes from procrastination. I can also show you missing pieces of my life, never to be repaired, because I let something important slide by.

Descriptions for being a procrastinator include attributes that no one should want attached to their personality or work ethic such as: lazy; move or act slow so as to fall behind; failure to maintain a speed set by others; delay in progress; aimless wasting of time; trifling or vacillation when promptness is necessary. These are not traits of someone who has taken charge of his or her life.

When helping others attack this devious disease of pro-crastination of putting off what should be dealt with front and center, you can probably use yourself as the best example, because you feel the strongest about your own experiences and your own emotions. I know I can.

Do you think you could help somebody attack procrasti-nation—develop the skill of going back, rehearsing your own life and come up with the essence of the emotion and the experience—to illustrate to somebody how insidious it can become and how devastating it can leave your life and what'll be missing if they let it slide? That is learning to attack the problem, for yourself and others. It's vital to go after the insid-ious in your life.

CONTEMPT VERSUS COMPASSION

A great Christian leader says, "The things I once hated, I now love. The things I once loved, I now hate." It's important to incorporate both love and hate in the same conversation when dealing with life.

Now, here's the dilemma. It's so easy to be careless with words and get the wrong reaction. What if you meant to say,

"What's troubling you?" And instead you said, "What's wrong with you?" Can you imagine the difference? Just the mistake of one small word means all the difference in the world and the kind of reaction and response you get in return.

So the dilemma is how to attack the problem, but not the person. God has the same dilemma. God says, "I love you, but I hate your sinful ways." That's a challenge, a problem, for us—to show people love while helping them destroy something hateful in their lives.

How do you put love and hate in the same sentence? It is essential to show your contempt for the problem and your concern for the value—your compassion for the person. These are not easy skills. You don't just walk with ease up these summits of intellectual thought and word choice and emotional content and precision. You don't learn this wisdom overnight,

Attack the problem— not the person.

but your commitment to excellence in communications can make all the difference in the world in how your economic and social and personal world works out.

And here's part of the challenge.

God says, "I love you, but I hate your sinful ways." Now, since me and my sinful ways are bound up so close together, I tend to take His statement personally. And God has to say, "No, no, no. Let me make it clear one more time. I love you, but I hate your sinful ways." He makes His intent clear. Just like you have to make it clear to your children, "I love you, but I hate what you're doing and what it's doing to you." Taking charge means learning how to put love and hate in the same sentence—making the insidious as devastating and as ominous as it should be, and make the opportunity and future as bright as it can be.

We must learn to paint by language and by emotions, how much we hate the wrong in order to develop the good. This truth is powerful, not something you can't be mild in acknowledging. For instance, you can't take a mild approach to the weeds in your garden. You must hate weeds bad enough to kill them.

You may say, "Well, I've learned to handle this stuff." This is not stuff you handle, this is stuff you devastate and eliminate. This is stuff you have to kill. If your treasure and value are in danger, you must go after the culprit with a high hatefulness by word, by language, by emotions, whatever's necessary to get the job done to reveal the evil and preserve the good.

These are not easy skills to learn, but if you want to extend your reach, in my opinion, you have to engage in the confrontation. It's where the values are exposed. Let me give you a good philosophical phrase, "All values must be won by

Secure and defend.

contest. And after they've been won, they must be defended." You may say, "Wow, you've put a pretty heavy task on us." That's what life is all about, a pretty heavy challenge. We don't give large trophies for small effort. If you want to experience good health, if you want to earn wealth, if you want to extend a long reach in touching people's lives, you have to engage in some extra powerful disciplines. One is to secure the territory by vigor, and the other is to defend it with equal challenge. Attack. Procrastination.

BLAME

Here's another problem we face, blame. I engaged in the "blame game" over a large portion of my life until I met Mr. Shoaff. I used to blame my negative relatives. I used to blame the government. I used to blame taxes. I used to blame prices.

I said, "It costs too much."

Shoaff said, "No, let's cover the real problem. You can't afford it."

I thought, *Wow, I never looked at it like that before.*

Shoaff said, "Sir, you must intellectually understand. *It's* not your problem. *You* are your problem."

It has been out there for about 6,000 years. You can't cure that. But what you *can* cure are errors in judgment, errors in attitude, errors in activity, errors in misjudging results. I finally realized that the errors were within, the blame is within. I appreciate that Mr. Shoaff went after me on that point.

EXCUSES

The next problem we need to attack are excuses. Wow, we have a million of them, one for every issue. "I'm too short, I'm too tall." "I'm too old, I'm too young." "I don't have the money." "I don't have the experience." On and on and on with the excuses. Learning to attack your excuses is crucial when taking charge of your life. I call these the "tools of last resort."

If you learn and use these skills, there's no telling who you can help. But you must save these for last, as the last resort. These are tools you don't use up front.

The first one is a *direct attack*. You have to be very careful of a direct attack so that it isn't misjudged in severity. Next is *scolding;* be very careful of scolding. Only use it as a last resort. For example, somebody walks in late and you say, "Where have you been?" That comment is loaded with insinuations, loaded. Again, be very careful, only use as a last resort. If you have to resort to it, you have to, but don't use it up front. Save a direct attack and scolding for when the occasion calls for such harsh language to go after a dire situation. The last one is *sarcasm*. Sarcasm can be useful, but save it for last. "Who do you think you are?" That's powerful language—save it for when it is meaningful to use such strong language.

Matters of the heart are delicate. Here's what we teach. Don't operate on the heart with a hatchet. When you use these tools, you have to be very careful to save the value and go after the problem. Now, let me give you the real clue. *The more you care, the stronger you can be.* People don't mind you using strong language about insidious things. They don't mind you becoming sharp, powerful, as long as you care.

And the more you care, the stronger you can be. I don't mind the minister consigning my soul to hellfire for my sinful ways. I don't mind that as long as he does it with tears, not

The more you care, the stronger you can be.

with joy. But wouldn't we all resist a dry-eyed sermon on hell-fire? I can't preach hellfire without my heart breaking. I sob my way through a sermon on hellfire—or I resist a dry-eyed attempt to preach on hellfire. Why? A simple, obvious lack of really caring.

And there are some subjects you can't even deal with unless your heart breaks and unless visibly it shows by the emotional content that you really care. Now you can deal harshly with some powerful, important problems. Tools of last resort. Attacking the problems but not the person.

OFFER SOLUTIONS

An exciting part of the human experience is the ability to paint results in advance. We call it borrowing from the future. But if you can't see the future, it makes today look pretty desperate. If you can't see the future, it makes your next step uncertain. Why bother to learn the skills and pay the price and go through all of the calisthenics and trials of learning and growing and changing, if you can't see the future reward? If there is no future, if there is no promise, why bother? So this is one of our great challenges in life—to paint for ourselves the upcoming times and to see the results in advance—borrowing from the future.

When you stop to think about it, planning and preparing and expecting a future reward is a tremendously unique experience. Being able to borrow from the future, bring it to the present, and use it as an incentive to get the job done today, to learn the skills and put those skills to work now for a planned future outcome is very satisfying, and profitable.

So painting results in advance—whether money results, whether position results, business possibilities, relationship opportunities, social, career, or ministry results—can lift your mindset, attitude, and be just the incentive you need to make those big moves toward being in charge of your life. Finding and executing solutions to problems along the way can be very powerful.

What makes the farmer work all spring and toil all summer? His vision of the harvest. If he couldn't see the harvest in advance, he wouldn't put the plow in the ground. If he couldn't visualize the opportunity, the chance to cash in and to turn wheat into money and money into lifestyle—if he couldn't see all that, why would he put the plow to the soil? He wouldn't.

Likewise, if you can't see the fruits of your labor, and if the promise of a good yield isn't clear, why put out the effort? You must paint for yourself the version of the future you desire that will motivate and maintain your enthusiasm for putting in the work to make it real.

In the same way, to get people to respond to what you propose, you have to paint for them a future that they will want to aspire to reach. They will want to put forth the effort, read the books, make the decisions, whatever it is. The key is to offer the solution and paint it clearly in their mind and emotions.

Jesus said to His disciples, in essence, "If you stick with me and believe in me and plant my teachings deep in your ideology and within your philosophy, if you walk the streets and pour your heart and soul into this work, you will never die. If you touch every human possible, cross the oceans, fling yourself on the known world, and spread the good news of what you have seen and heard the last three and a half years,

I promise you, after you have finished this rather difficult task of putting all of your energy, time, and effort into your mission, I promise you that in my Father's house are many mansions. And where I am you will be." Wow.

And His disciples did indeed cross the oceans, walk the streets, and touch every human they could touch. They put every ounce of energy and mind and soul and spirit into His philosophy, right up until the time most of them forfeited their life for the opportunity. No wonder those teachings have been passed along for more than 2,000 years, and counting.

The picture of the future that Jesus painted for His disciples had the promise of a grand home with Him. Wouldn't you put effort into a task if somebody credible told you about such a unique promise? And the answer is, yes, of course. All we have to do is see the promise clearly enough, and we will do amazing things.

SUMMARY

By way of review, we've been covering the major parts in a presentation of communicating effectively whether to a child or a business audience or a sales situation. Everyone has the opportunity to affect others with words. A presentation of any type can be divided into four important parts: identification; logic and reason; attack the problem; offer solutions.

Identification. Learning how to relate to other people is pretty easy if they are all like you. Otherwise it can be difficult getting to know people who aren't like you. If there's a difference in color, religion, age, experience, and or background, establishing a relationship can get a little more complicated—but it can be mastered. All you have to do is refine the skills you have learned in this book to have a longer reach economically, socially, and personally. Deal in subjects that make you real. Tell your story with authority.

Logic and reason. Brevity is key, don't offer too many facts. There are probably thousands of facts about an automobile, but you don't need to share all of them for people to make their decision. About six or eight will do. And if you stretch it beyond the half dozen, you may lose your audience. So keep it brief when it comes to logic and reason.

Attack the problems. When mounting an offense against a problem, attack the problem—not the person.

Offer solutions. To offer solutions to a problem is like painting results in advance.

5

THE ART OF PERSUASION

Now let's engage in a very exciting subject—the art of persuasion. I found there's a great deal of difference between presentation and persuasion. When I first got into sales, I became a pretty good presenter. Mr. Shoaff taught me well. I heard people say, "I've listened to a lot of salesmen, but you have to be one of the best." I thought, *Wow, the man has taught me well.* Somebody else would say, "Hey, I've been around. I think I've heard them all, but wow, you have to be the best. You're one of the greatest salesmen I've ever heard." And I thought, *Wow, I've learned this stuff pretty quickly.*

Then one day the awful truth dawned on me, I thought, *Hey, wait a minute. Something's wrong here. If I'm one of the world's all-time great salesmen, how come they ain't buying?* Wow. I started to realize that I had an additional skill to learn. Although I was very good at *presentation.* I had yet to get good at *persuasion.*

Two great orators, or speakers, of antiquity are Demosthenes, a Greek and Cicero, a Roman. But it was said of Cicero when he spoke, "What a great speech." It was said of Demosthenes when he spoke, "Let us march." And that's the difference between presentation and persuasion.

To take charge of your life, I'm asking you to learn this additional skill. You a good persuader if the results follow the presentation.

Passion, emotion, beliefs, convictions—if you learn to articulate those parts of you well, you will get the results you want. If you learn to let all those traits flow, not just from the surface but from down deep from a lifetime of experience, you will get positive results. If you draw from all of those feelings and commitments and awareness, even some misgivings, even not knowing it all, even with a sense of humility—that flow of emotions seals the point in the final art of persuasion.

So let's talk about the art of persuasion, what all it entails, and why it's important.

BE A GOOD STORYTELLER

If you're involved in a company that deals in numbers and business and products and volume of business, make sure you translate all the business into stories. Sometimes it's easy to say, "We did $10 million in business last month." And then we forget the stories that are involved in that $10 million.

So here's what I'm asking you to do. Become story conscious as well as figure conscious. How many stories does $10 million represent? Many, no doubt. But if you're only interested in the numbers, not the stories, you limit your outreach. Use your newfound skills of communication to tell the stories behind the figures—people love to hear stories. Translate activity and business and volume and money and numbers into people, into people's lives and stories, and all who are involved in the transactions.

Become your own best storyteller. Learn to tell your own story, whether it's identification, logic, solutions, be a student of your own life. It's so important to go back over your own life.

At the end of each day, it's good to review your experiences. This is *learning to reflect.* One of the keys of making the past more valuable to invest in the future is learning how to reflect. Take a few minutes at the end of the day and think about the day. Who did you see and who did you meet and who did you talk to and what happened? Why did they say what they said and why did you say what you said? We call this "running the tapes again."

Reflecting on the past makes investing in the future more valuable.

When you take a few minutes at the end of the day and run the tapes of the day again, that day will take a more important place in your equity future. You can draw from that day. But if you casually go through the day and miss the opportunity to lock that day into your consciousness, sure enough, at some future time when you could have drawn from that experience, it won't be available.

Here's how to lock in your past and make it more of an equity.

Take a few hours at the end of the week to go back over the week. A week is a good chunk of time. Think about the sights and the sounds and the colors and the people and the decisions and the mistakes and the errors and the successes. Review the week and let what happened take a more powerful place in your awareness.

Also, I encourage you to take a half day at the end of each month to review the month as a whole. A month is a really good chunk of time. We wouldn't let a company's progress and records to go by without reviewing at least every 30 days. Your life is just as or more important as a company—don't be casual about taking a look back over the events at work, home, and socially.

I'm asking you not to let your life go more than about 30 days without taking a serious look at the numbers and the situations and the joys and the traumas—what you've done and what you've said and how you've grown in your experiences. That one 30-day period takes a stronger place in your memory, and may make a difference, have an impact later in your life.

Take a weekend at the end of the year and call it your time to reflect on the past year. Why? To make the past more valuable. If you treat your life experiences as valuable they can become commodity, currency, resources. Why try to make the past more valuable? Here's the simple answer—to invest it in your future.

When my father was about to turn 76 years old, I said to him, "Dear father, can you imagine the incredible experiences that are waiting for you to gather up from the last 75 years of your life and invest them into your 76th?"

That's a huge difference in the way to look at aging. Most people just try and make it through from year to year. Let me offer you this challenge: gather up more of your past and invest it in your future. Part of that gathering is studying your own story, which could be so powerful in identifying issues and offering answers and solutions. No telling what amazing opportunities may be revealed if you took a little time to uncover what you haven't thought about or talked about for a while. If you were to dig back, there's no telling what additional stories and experiences you could reawaken, so that when the opportunity comes, you can draw from that experience and invest it into that conversation. You may be very surprised at who you could touch, and how many it may touch. Without that digging and reliving, you may have missed that opportunity to touch, to reach out.

Stories, your stories, other people's stories. A great way to illustrate facts and ideas and philosophy is to use the stories of life, because that's the real stuff of life. The stories of life.

DEAL IN TRUTH, ACCURATE FACTS

In the art of persuasion, you must provide accurate facts, also known as dealing in truth. Accuracy is very important because it builds credibility. Credibility starts to weaken and can be totally discredited if you mess with the facts, the truth, the correct numbers.

Most people will give you room for what we call an unintentional or slight error in dealing in facts. For example, if my watch shows 7:28, but when you asked me what time is it and I said 7:30, you would allow me to be a couple of minutes off. I wasn't in no way leading you astray with this erroneous information that it was 7:30 when really it was only 7:28.

But there are times and occasions when you may have to be precise; it may be a life and death. Generally speaking, people will give you room for making an unintentional error in stating the truth. Beyond a sort of reasonableness of unintentional error, we get into an area in higher circles that is considered unacceptable. Some people deal in exaggeration that eventually destroys their credibility.

Never destroy your credibility.

For example, if you are giving testimony in a trial and you're on the witness stand, if you are caught telling a lie, guess what they do with the rest of your testimony? They throw it all away. Why? You have destroyed your credibility. The guy on the stand says, "Well, no, I only lied just that one time." Well, how are we going to believe that? All it takes is one lie to weaken and actually nullify your whole testimony.

Therefore, a key in the art of persuasion to deal in truth and fact.

True sophistication in speaking and writing is the total absence of exaggeration. Exaggeration is the childish attempt to make up for lack of self-worth. If you don't feel adequate, more often than not, you tend to deal in exaggerations to make up in numbers what you may lack in character or what you lack in substance or what you lack in confidence.

But if you build character and confidence and precision of thinking and decision making, and you have a sense of growing worth and value, you don't mind dealing in absolute truth and accuracy because that's what counts.

Factual accuracy and telling the truth are absolutes. After all, you never know who's going to be around to check the accuracy of your stories. For example:

In one of my weekend leadership series sessions, I was talking about a murder trial I attended many, many years prior that took place in Houston, Texas. I was describing the murder trial scene and the lawyer who turned down the case, then they hired another lawyer to defend the Black man who had killed a bus driver. Someone told me it was going to be quite a dramatic trial and I should go. I happened to be in the area, so I went. I was there every day and the Black lawyer from Dallas was so brilliant. I was swept away by his language and his style and his uniqueness. He had the whole court-room mesmerized.

So I'm telling this whole story in class for some illustration I was using and when I finished the story, a lady stood up. There were about 40 to 50 people in class. She stood up and said, "Mr. Rohn, may I say something?"

I said, "Yes, of course."

She turned around to face the group and said, "Ladies and gentlemen, I've just had a unique experience. This story that Mr. Rohn told you about the murder trial in Houston, Texas, some fifteen years ago, I want you to know the experience I've had in listening to the story has been unique because I was there."

She said, "The attorney who turned down the case, a pretty famous attorney, happened to be my boss. I was his legal secretary. I also sat in that courtroom. I want you to know Mr. Rohn has described to you exactly what happened."

And I thought, *Wow, that was close*. So, tell accurate stories and deal in truth because you never know when 15 years later someone may be sitting in your audience. Learn to trust the truth. There's nothing more powerful than the truth.

Here's another ancient quote that rings true then, now, and always: The truth will set you free. What sets you free? The truth. Many people are dealing in affirmations, but I'll tell you what sets you free is the truth. It's best to affirm the truth. If you're broke, affirm that you're broke. That's what you put up on the refrigerator. The truth sets you free.

BETTER UNDERSTATED THAN OVERSTATED

The next key in the art of persuasion—better to be understated than overstated. I wrote a book titled *Seasons of Life* and my picture is in it. It isn't the best picture. The book came out about three years ago. I published it myself. Every once in a while, somebody says, "Mr. Rohn, this picture of you in your book *Seasons of Life* is not the greatest picture of you." I say, "I know, that's why it's in there, so that when I show up I look better than the picture."

A lot of people use glamour Hollywood-type photos. And when they show up in person, they look a little used around the edges, right? I'd rather have people surprised on the upside than surprised on the disappointing side.

One of the greatest lessons I've learned when working with people is to let them find out the end result was more than you promised and easier than you said. Later, you always want people to be pleasantly surprised. The key here is to learn to trust the truth. If the truth doesn't seem to be enough for some people, then all you need is to become stronger yourself in presenting the truth.

And you need to face the truth as well. Only when you acknowledge the truth about yourself will you look for ways to make life better. For example, when you're getting ready for the day, if you're broke, admit it. There's nothing better to set you free than the sometimes cold, hard facts, the truth. So deal in truth.

Affirmation without discipline leads to the delusion of not accurately assessing your situation. You say, "Well, that's a bit negative." Sometimes life comes with negativity. You have to deal with it. If your car isn't running quite right, do you pretend it's working perfectly—or do you take it to a mechanic to assess the problem and then give you a truthful cause and solution to fix the problem?

Living a delusional life is not living in the real world at all. Take to find out what's really wrong, admit it, and then take the necessary steps to turn negativity into a positive outcome. Take your car to as many mechanics it takes to find the full extent of the facts of the negative problem. When you know the truth, you can deal with truth. You can deal with the problem. You can act on the positive outcome; but at first you have to know the problem before you can find the answer. So dealing in truth about any and all issues or problems is so important, it sets you free.

BORROW

Next in the list of key elements to remember in the art of persuasion is to borrow from others. What do I mean by that? If someone has made a great statement or observation, using language that you find commendable and worthy of sharing to illustrate a point, you might as well borrow it. I borrow everything I can borrow, always careful to give full credit to the originator of the quote.

All the wisdom Mr. Shoaff taught me, I borrow and share as much of all that as possible. Of course, I give him credit for all he shared with me. Some people have said it so well, there's no use trying to think up another way to say it. When you use credible and notable quotes, it also shows your audience that

Always deal in truth.

you've done your homework. It shows you're passionately interested in your subject.

The quotes, the stories of adventures, tragedies, and triumphs that people have experienced are what connect people. In some seminars I use a lot of quotes when I'm talking about humans being affected by each other. I even quote the lyrics from songs. One such: "If not for you, the winter would hold no spring, couldn't hear a robin sing. I just wouldn't have a clue if not for you." That's so well said; I couldn't improve much on that. So the key is to just borrow, borrow all that you can borrow to support your argument, to express your heart, or to express your mind and your feelings. This is part of the art of persuasion. Learning to borrow from someone else that has been well-said and well-constructed—while always giving credit where credit is due.

Winston Churchill said, "The truth is incontrovertible. Malice may attack it and ignorance may deride it, but in the end, there it is." See, that's so well said. You could stay up all night and not think of that, but you don't have to stay up all night and think of it. Churchill already said it. That statement, that definition of truth is so powerful and it's so brief and it's so precise and it's so dramatic that you might as well borrow the drama that comes from the language he spoke by exercising the quote.

I talk about the brevity of life in one of my other lectures. The Beatles sang a song titled "We Can Work it Out," in which are the lyrics: "Life is very short, and there's no time for fussing and fighting, my friend...." What powerful words, especially considering that for John Lennon on the streets of New York, his life was cut extra short. Those are powerful words. Elton John sang, "She lived her life like a candle in the wind." Wow,

Words are powerful.

I can't think of much better lyrics to describe how fragile life is and how brief it is.

Words can be arranged uniquely that will capture the attention and move an entire diverse group of people as well as an individual. The key is to learn the words and see what you can do with them. You have a special way of looking at the world, events, people, nature, etc. that you can put to words which will move, touch, and affect others.

You can also borrow the words, borrow the quotes of other people to support your expressions, your communication, your conversations. Benjamin Disraeli, two-time prime minister of the United Kingdom, said, "Nothing can resist a human will that will stake its existence on its purpose." Wow, that's a powerful statement. We call this towering language. We call this climbing the summit of words and sentences and phrases that have incredible meaning, so briefly said and yet so powerfully done. You might as well borrow the power and borrow the explanation and borrow the effect of somebody else's unique words when you realize that you couldn't say it better.

Borrow quotes or observances from credible and admirable people, past and present, and use them into your presentation and conversations and you will see a dramatic difference in your audience's response right away.

Even US President John F. Kennedy noted the British prime minister's gift of using words to his and the world's advantage. Kennedy said, "Winston Churchill had the ability in World War II to take the English language and send it into battle. And we were all inspired by the speeches rallied to the cause, the tenacity to hang on the visions of the rascal Hitler and his insidious casting a long shadow over the land of

Europe. Churchill had the ability to use the language to get us to see and to get us to think and to stir the mind and stir the heart and stir the soul."

Words are so formidable, so use words of your own that are powerful; but when you need it, reach out and borrow someone else's words who has said it well and offer it for others to consider, to touch the heart and touch the soul and mend the problem and help someone to decide to move, to change, to grow.

Of course, this isn't an easy task. The art of persuasion isn't meant to be easy. It means paying a price, because that's how you appreciate the promise of language, the language that affects the cure, the language that reaches and touches. You have to learn these skills, learn the craft, and then you will change yourself and others who see the value in what you have to say.

ORATORY DRAMA

Oratory is a dramatic way of speaking to catch someone's attention, to drive the point home. You may not have much use for oratory, but it is good to explore the word. I probably use more oratory informally than I do in public. I'm a little more reserved on the platform behind a podium. I get a little more dramatic person-to-person. It's just my style. A little more conservative in public, a little more dramatic in person. But I do have a bit of experience in oratory.

In one of my lectures, I go through a whole list called the "Diseases of Attitude," and when I get to the last one, which is complaining, I really want to make my point clear. I say with authority and confidently, "Spend five minutes complaining and you have wasted five and you may have begun what's known as economic cancer of the bone. They will soon haul you off into a financial desert and there you will choke on the dust of your own regret." Now, that's what we call a bit of oratory. A dramatic burst of proclamation. Now don't do 30 minutes of that. That would be too much; but when the occasion calls for oratory, saying something in a more dramatic fashion, then by all means use it.

STRAIGHT TALK

The next one is very important when perfecting the art of persuasion—straight talk. Or in other words, tell it like it is. Or, "Level with me." Straight talk means to put it on the line, say what you mean, what's the bottom line, where the rubber meets the road, and similar catch phrases.

Straight talk was one of the great experiences I had in meeting this incredible gentleman, Mr. Shoaff, when I was 25 years old. As mentioned previously, Mr. Shoaff attended school only to the eighth grade, so he advised me in very simple language—he laid it on the line. One day he said, "Mr. Rohn, if you're 25 years old and you're an American male and you've been to high school and one year of college and you're not at least a third of your way toward your fortune," he said, "isn't something wrong?"

I'd never looked at my life like that before, as being wrong. He said, "Something's wrong." Then he said, "There's nothing wrong with the country and nothing wrong with the companies and there's nothing wrong with the banks and the money—but there's something wrong with your plan. There's nothing wrong with you, but there's something wrong with your thinking, something wrong with your plan. You bought the wrong story, you bought the wrong formula, and it's easy to wind up a nice person and broke. It's easy to wind up sincere and poor. I'm telling you, you can be sincere and poor and you can work hard and be poor if you buy the wrong formula, buy the wrong plan. You didn't add up the percentages, you never took out the calculator, you never counted the cost as an ancient phrase says."

That blunt, straight-talk language really helped uncover my problem. That was one of the most clear-cut, sharply defined pieces of advice he gave me that helped change my life for the better.

In another of my lectures, I deal with the basics, the fundamentals of life and getting ahead and becoming successful. There are only a few fundamentals—there are no new fundamentals. Beware of somebody who says, "I have new fundamentals." No. Fundamentals are old. For example, you have to be suspicious of a guy who says, "We're manufacturing antiques." Ha!

One of the greatest basic fundamental comes from an ancient Bible phrase, "Whatever you sow, you will reap." We simply call this the law of sowing and reaping.

Continuing, Mr. Shoaff said to me, "Mr. Rohn, there's another way to quote this law that may very well help you discover where the problem lies."

I said, "Okay, I'm ready."

He said, "Whatever you reap is what you have sown."

I thought, *Wow, I never thought about that. Now there goes my list of all the things and people I blamed for my current circumstances.*

If you don't like the crop, who do you look for? Answer. Whoever planted it. And where do you find who planted your crop? Answer. In the mirror. Come fall, come harvest time, you go to the mirror and if necessary you say, "A few skinny carrots. I'm unimpressed. Where were you last spring? Asleep. Didn't you read the books? Did you break your hoe?"

This type of self-examination is called being straightforward, an uncomplicated truthful look at where you are. This is talking straight. This is telling it like it is. Along these same lines, you may want to ask yourself: "Am I reading enough books or am I not? If I engage in my current financial practices, will it take me toward the fortune I hope for in the next ten years or will it not? If I keep up my current health practices, will I have the vitality and the health and the vigor to do all the things I want to do five years from now? Will I or won't I? Are my current practices taking me where I would really like to go or have I been kidding myself for quite some time?"

As mentioned in a previous chapter, there was a day just before I met Mr. Shoaff that I called "Do Not Kid Myself Anymore" day. There was no use Mickey Mousing with the numbers. There was no use trying to stretch it. There was no use trying to excuse it. There was no use trying to paint it some phony color. I had to tell it like it is because it's the truth that starts the freedom mechanism working. It's the truth that will relieve the mind of all the guilt and all the excuses and brings you face to face about the actual problem.

When I finally discovered that the government wasn't my problem and that prices weren't my problem and the company and company policy wasn't the problem and my negative relatives and the weather and the economy and the community weren't the problem—when I finally discovered it was me, we call that trauma.

After I accepted the truth and passed through the trauma of discovering that it was me, not all the other things I'd blamed all those years, it suddenly dawned on me, "Hey, if it's me, if I'm the cause of the problem, I can do something about that right away!" And I got excited after my trauma had passed.

I realized that if the problem was the government, prices, or other people, there is probably not much of a chance any of that is going to change any time soon, if ever. It's going to be about like it's always been, right? Opportunity mixed with difficulty. So if all those things are going to remain in place

"I can do something about that right away!"

the next few years, which I imagine they will, the only change that is really going to dramatically affect my life is me.

Now put yourself in my place. Have you been blaming others or other things for your situation? Is there anyone or anything causing your problems? Or is the cause of your circumstances the person you see in the mirror?

Mr. Shoaff said to me, "Mr. Rohn, if it isn't going well for you, don't ask what's wrong out there. You ask, what's wrong in here?" He pointed to his chest, his heart. There's a Black heritage spiritual hymn that says, "It's not my mother nor my father. It's not my brother nor my sister. It's me." What a revelation.

When you find out it's you who have created your current state, then you can go to work making changes that very day—today. You can start stretching today. You can start reading new books today. You can sign up for new classes today. You can start engaging in constructive thinking today. You can make life-changing decisions today. You never have to be the same again—it's your choice, your decision to make.

So while you wait for prices to come down and government reform to happen and while you wait for the outside to change, go to work immediately on the refinement of your own thinking and the refinement of your own disciplines, and watch how quickly your personal equity starts to grow. This is called dealing in straight talk.

When a father who is 40 and broke living in this country finally discovers he is the problem, when his children say, "Daddy, how come we're not rich?" he can speak the truth and say, "I'll tell you why we don't have money. I smoked it. I wasted it. I spent our financial resources in small daily pieces on nothing important. I didn't realize how my spending would mount up to be a fortune over the past 20 years. To be honest with you, I spent our fortune on nonessentials. Somehow I fell for all the gimmicks and didn't realize the price I was going to pay in the future." This is called dealing in truth, straight talk, telling it like it is—so you can make changes and start fresh, right where you are today to take charge of your life.

CHALLENGES

Next to discuss in the art of persuasion are the challenges that we face in life and our response to a challenge. I don't know any human being who doesn't respond to a challenge. From the time we were small and someone asked, "How high can you jump? How fast can you run? How much can you do? Can you win?" We all face challenges throughout our lives, so part of the art of persuasion is the variety of ways we respond.

One of the greatest challenges Mr. Shoaff gave me was when he said, "Let's go do it." That's a great challenge—not, you go do it. *Let's* go do it.

It's easy to say, "You go do it. You go change your life, you go be successful, you go make the decisions." But how much better if somebody comes along and says, "Let's go do it. Let's read the extra books. Let's make the decisions, let's pour it on for the next six months. Let's go full speed, 110 percent and see what comes of that."

What an inspiring jolt of motivation we get when someone says, "Let's go do it!" That's the greatest of challenges.

Much of life is a challenge—everyone knows that. From the boss asking for statistics at the last minute before a big

Let's tackle that challenge together!

meeting to your child wanting attention in the middle of an important phone call, each challenge presents a unique set of circumstances. Therefore, it is vital to articulate the challenge when the push is on so you can respond accordingly. That's what life is all about. Accepting the challenges, driving the roots deep, becoming as strong as possible, and understanding that whatever comes your way, you can make it into an opportunity for your benefit.

Attempting your best, trying your hardest, thinking well, reading well, living well, struggling with all that lands at your doorstep, that's called the challenge—but that's exactly what makes life worthwhile. That's where the value is, the struggle for high ideals to make something unique out of your life. I don't know how better to put it—the challenge. Look at each one as a piece of the puzzle of life—the life you are in charge of.

The last aspect of the art of persuasion is passion. Passion is the emotion behind persuasion.

The unique thing about emotions is that emotions give us the drive to act. Emotions are the spirit within us. Emotions put the life in what we do, say, think, react. It isn't just knowledge that makes you wealthy. It's knowledge mixed with feelings and attitudes and emotions. The surge of feelings and emotions can be overwhelming at times. So the key is to know that our emotions need to be educated. We have to school and control our emotions for them to be most beneficial.

We call civilization the intelligent management of human emotions. You may have the drive and the power to get anywhere you want to go, but without well-educated and well-directed emotions, you will make no progress. Outbursts

Civilization is the intelligent management of human emotions.

and wild behavior instigated by uncurbed emotions turn good intentions into disastrous situations.

There is a fine line between passion and undefined emotion. What it takes to perfect the art of persuasion, is putting yourself into the picture—allowing the audience to see and feel your passion, emotion, beliefs, and convictions. When you learn to articulate those well, and let those inherent traits flow not just from the surface but from down deep, from a lifetime of experience, you will have the power to persuade. When you draw from your feelings and commitments and awareness, even misgivings with a sense of humility, the outcome will be stupendous—for you *and* your audience.

Your flow of directed emotion seals the point in the final art of persuasion, when people have picked up that you really believe and are committed to what you've been talking about. That's why you laid it on the line. That's why you borrowed essential quotes. That's why you said it as well as you could say it. That's why you told every story you could. That's why you used yourself front and center—because you so passionately believe in the moment and what you're trying to accomplish in the way of decision making in touching somebody else's life.

Now, how good can you get at the art of persuasion? One of the best illustrations I can give you is an ancient Bible story, dramatically told, in essence, as follows:

> *King Agrippa was advised one day that there was a famous man in his prison. They came and said, "Oh, King Agrippa, we have the man you've been wanting to capture for a long time. We have him locked up in your dungeon." King Agrippa knew*

Lay it all on the line.

who the man was. He was the great leader of the early Christians, formerly known as Saul from Tarsus, now known as Paul, apostle leader of the early Christians.

King Agrippa was brought this incredible news that this man is in his dungeon and he may have said, "You mean the man himself is in my prison?" They said, "Oh yes, King, we got the man." Agrippa evidently had studied the whole Christian movement and had watched it grow to an unacceptable size. And evidently he knew a lot about the Paul. "Bring him to me. I have to see the man in person," demanded the king.

So they hauled him out of the dungeon and stood the man in front of the king. King Agrippa took one look at him and said, "Paul, I've heard all about you. Now you find yourself in my dungeon. Tell me what is going on. What is this Christian movement? Why are all these people willing to give their lives for this incredible cause and willing to sacrifice themselves? It's growing like a prairie fire, spreading like wildfire." The king persists, saying, "What's happening? What is this Christian thing? What about you? What's your involvement? Tell me your story."

The king shouldn't have asked, because Paul was ready to explain, with eloquence, precision, drama, passion, and truth. If you're a reader of drama and stories, this is one of the most important speeches to read in all of literature and history. Paul gave the greatest example of someone who knew how to use the language to tell his story—his life-changing, eternal life story.

Then Agrippa said to Paul, "You may speak in your defense."

So Paul, gesturing with his hand, started his defense: "I am fortunate, King Agrippa, that you are the one hearing my defense today against all these accusations made by the Jewish leaders, for I know you are an expert on all Jewish customs and controversies. Now please listen to me patiently!

"As the Jewish leaders are well aware, I was given a thorough Jewish training from my earliest childhood among my own people and in

Jerusalem. If they would admit it, they know that I have been a member of the Pharisees, the strictest sect of our religion. Now I am on trial because of my hope in the fulfillment of God's promise made to our ancestors. In fact, that is why the twelve tribes of Israel zealously worship God night and day, and they share the same hope I have. Yet, Your Majesty, they accuse me for having this hope! Why does it seem incredible to any of you that God can raise the dead?

"I used to believe that I ought to do everything I could to oppose the very name of Jesus the Nazarene. Indeed, I did just that in Jerusalem. Authorized by the leading priests, I caused many believers there to be sent to prison. And I cast my vote against them when they were condemned to death. Many times I had them punished in the synagogues to get them to curse Jesus. I was so violently opposed to them that I even chased them down in foreign cities.

"One day I was on such a mission to Damascus, armed with the authority and commission of the leading priests. About noon, Your Majesty, as I was on the road, a light from heaven brighter than the sun shone down on me and my companions. We all fell down, and I heard a voice saying to me in Aramaic, 'Saul, Saul, why are you persecuting me? It is useless for you to fight against my will.'

"'Who are you, lord?' I asked.

"And the Lord replied, 'I am Jesus, the one you are persecuting. Now get to your feet! For I have appeared to you to appoint you as my servant and witness. Tell people that you have seen me, and tell them what I will show you in the future. And I will rescue you from both your own people and the Gentiles. Yes, I am sending you to the Gentiles to open their eyes, so they may turn from darkness to light and from the power of Satan to God. Then they will receive forgiveness for their sins and be given a place among God's people, who are set apart by faith in me.'

"And so, King Agrippa, I obeyed that vision from heaven. I preached first to those in Damascus, then in Jerusalem and throughout all Judea, and also to the Gentiles, that all must repent of their sins and turn to God—and prove they have changed by the good things they do. Some Jews arrested me in the Temple for preaching this, and they tried to kill me. But God has protected me right up to this present time so I can testify to everyone, from the least to the greatest. I teach nothing except what the prophets and Moses said would happen—that the Messiah would suffer and be the first to rise from the dead, and in this way announce God's light to Jews and Gentiles alike."

Suddenly, Festus shouted, "Paul, you are insane. Too much study has made you crazy!"

But Paul replied, "I am not insane, Most Excellent Festus. What I am saying is the sober truth. And King Agrippa knows about these things. I speak boldly, for I am sure these events are all familiar to him, for they were not done in a corner! King Agrippa, do you believe the prophets? I know you do—"

Agrippa interrupted him. "Do you think you can persuade me to become a Christian so quickly?"

Paul replied, "Whether quickly or not, I pray to God that both you and everyone here in this audience might become the same as I am, except for these chains." (Acts 26:1-29)

What a drama. What a perfect example of the art of persuasion and communication.

Well, you may never have the chance to persuade a king but you may get as good as presenting yourself to an audience and make a life-changing impact.

Communications, touching people with words, using your talents, skills, and experiences to make a difference in people's lives is a worthy endeavor. Touching people with words comes out in numbers as about 20 percent of what you know, and 80 percent of how you feel. So I ask you to work on knowledge, yes, of course, but the greatest of skills is to work on the precision of emotions, feelings, commitment, passion for the cause, for the occasion to solve a problem, to touch somebody truly with spirit, as well as mind, with heart, as well as words.

6

BE SOMEBODY

In the quest to take charge of your life, I call *leadership* the challenge to be something more than mediocre, the step-up to the new challenge, taking every new opportunity. In this chapter we will be discussing leadership skills.

It was said of Abraham Lincoln, "He was at his mother's bedside when she died, and her last words were, 'Be somebody, Abe.'" And if that story is true, evidently he took it to heart and proceeded from that moment to become somebody, which is the key to leadership—inner inspection of your gifts and your skills, your integrity, and your character. Here's a good phrase for you to jot down: to attract attractive people, you must be attractive.

Now we return to the central theme of all of my lectures—the most significant aspect of your world starts with you. Mr. Shoaff gave me in dramatic fashion another one of the major keys that changed my life. He said, "Work harder on yourself than you do on your job." That simple statement started to make measurable changes in my life in a fairly short period of time. I had discovered up until age 25, that I had worked hard on my job but not on myself—which was my reason for lack of progress.

To attract attractive people, you must be attractive.

When it comes to being a leader, the same thing applies. If you really want to attract attractive people, if you'd like to have people of quality be part of your life, the key is to become a person of quality yourself.

Leadership is the ability to attract someone to the gifts, skills, and opportunities that surround you as a person, manager, professional, coworker—a leader. I call leadership the great challenge of the ages in a wide variety of areas, science, politics, industry, education, sales, and especially parenting. Sometimes parents don't see themselves as leaders, but being a parent offers the greatest possibility to influence children and young people. Exhibiting leadership qualities takes you to high levels of success and opens doors to many new and exciting opportunities and experiences.

In addition to self-introspection of your gifts, skills, integrity, and character, a self-inspection of your outer look is also necessary when assuming leadership roles. How do you present yourself to others? Are you as confident and knowledgeable as you appear to be? Do you reflect your inner strengths? The inside and the outside are both of equal importance.

When you first meet someone, right away they will take a look at you. Sure they're going to listen, but while they do they're also taking a look. Certainly we learn to evaluate people by more than what we see, but at first we naturally look at their physical appearance, clothing, hair, shoes. An ancient phrase says, "People look on the outside; God looks on the inside." That's an excellent truth. So that might mean work on the inside for God, work on the outside for people. You say, "Well, people shouldn't judge me by my appearance." Well, that may be—but they absolutely do. They do judge by your

Your inside and your outside are equally important.

appearance. You can't deal in shoulds and shouldn'ts. You must deal in realities.

When people get to know you, they will judge you by more than what they see, but at first it's all they have to go by—what they see and what they hear. Sure there's more to come, but at first you have to pass the initial meet and greet test.

VICTORIOUS ATTRIBUTES FOR EVERY CHALLENGE

The challenge to be somebody comes with certain attributes to meet that challenge. The following is a brief list.

- *Be somebody wise*. There's no substitute for smart. Threats don't make up for smart. Volume and shouting

Learn to deal in realities.

don't make up for smart. There's no substitute for smart.

- *Be somebody strong.* Strength is attractive, and there are many ways to be strong—in decision making, character, language. As well as vitality and health. There are a lot of strengths, and they're all attractive.

- *Be strong, not rude,* which is a refinement of leadership skills. Some people mistake rudeness for strength. It's not even a good substitute.

- *Be kind, not weak.* We must not mistake weakness for kindness, because kindness isn't weak. Kindness is a certain kind of strength. We must be kind enough to tell somebody the truth. We must be kind enough and considerate enough to lay it on the line. We must be kind enough to tell it like it is and not deal in delusions. That's kindness, not weakness.

- *Be bold, not a bully.* It take boldness to win the day, to become a leader. You have to stride out front. You have to be willing to take the first arrows. You have to be willing to take the first problem, first trouble, leading the way. You must boldly seize the spring. Farming is not an easy task, it's hard work. It's hard work planting the seed, letting it grow at its own pace, defending it against all encroachments of bugs and weeds. No, it is not an easy task—but it's one of the best illustrations I know of life. If you want any value at all come harvest, you have to work hard and be bold. You have to seize each opportunity. The high life is not for the timid or the shy.

- *Be humble, not timid.* Some people mistake timidity for humility, but humility is a virtue. Timidity is a disease. It's a malady. It's an affliction. Now, it can be cured, but it is a problem. On the other hand, humility is an almost God-like word, a sense of awe, wonder, dimension, understanding the distance in worth and value and awareness of the human soul, the spirit; it's something unique about the human drama versus the rest of life. Humility is a grasp of the distance between us and the stars, and yet having the feeling that we are part of the stars.

- *Be thoughtful, not lazy*. It's okay to dream, but don't become only a dreamer.

- *Be proud, not arrogant*—a good refinement attribute. It takes healthy pride to win the day. Good leaders take pride in company, philosophy, opportunity, in community and school, laudable group organizations, in cause and accomplishment. But the key is to be proud without being arrogant. Do you know the worst kind of arrogance? Arrogance from ignorance. It's intolerable.

- *Deal in realities, deal in truth*. Save yourself the agony. Just accept that it is what it is. Life is fairly unique. Accept it is unique. Some people call it tragic, but it's best to call it unique. The black widow spider eats her mate after he's finished his noble task. Some people call that awful. I think it's more important to call it unique. The whole drama of life is unique, right?

The Bible is one of the most fascinating books to read because it is so unique in its presentation. One story says that God and satan were chatting away one day. I wouldn't have

Accept life as unique.

thought that was possible. Isn't that unique? As they're chatting away, they look down at what's happening on earth. Now, that's unique. I thought, *How often do they get together, and chat, and talk about stuff?* I don't know the answer, but the drama of the story is absolutely fascinating, unique.

On this particular occasion, the story says that God started bragging about one of his favorite people, Job. He told satan that Job was honest, rich, abhorred evil, and loved the Lord his God. He told satan that He was taking good care of His friend, Job.

Finally, satan had enough of hearing about how wonderful Job was. He said to God that Job was a great man because God had built a wall of protection around him and satan couldn't get to him in his normal fashion—couldn't tempt, harass, and cause him pain.

I find this conversation fascinating, unique.

Then satan told God that if He took down the special wall of protection from around Job so that satan could work his evil, Job would curse God to His face, and then die.

God told satan Job would never do that. Job was His special friend.

So satan challenged God.

Wow, isn't that a uniquely fascinating scenario?

Job doesn't know anything about this conversation.

God told satan he could do what he wanted with Job—but not kill him. Satan agreed and promised God that Job would end up cursing God. But God was certain that Job would remain faithful.

According to the story (found in the book of Job in the Bible), God removed the wall of protection and satan began his evil work. First, he caused his entire family to die, except Job's wife. Next, Job's servants and livestock were killed or taken by nearby enemies. Nevertheless, Job maintained his integrity and didn't curse God.

So then satan caused Job to suffer with painful sores all over his body. Satan afflicted Job with a triple blow—destroying his family, fortune, and health. In one of the last scenes of the story, Job is sitting on the ashes—everything gone, and he is scraping his sores with a rock. His wife comes along—seeing him sitting there and knowing what all had happened—and said to Job, "It looks like your Friend God has forsaken you. Why don't you just curse Him and die!"

Satan surely thinks this is when it will happen—this is when Job will curse God. But not so.

In the last chapter in the book of Job—after his wife and friends had derided him—Job still did not curse God. Then the Lord restored his family, fortune, and health. God blessed Job's life even more than what he had before. Job lived 140 years more and saw four generations of his children and grandchildren. Job became, according to history, one of the richest, most powerful men in the known world.

Your life may never become as desperate as what Job faced, but it certainly can be frustrating at times. We can learn to turn frustration into fascination, though, right? You can give up trying to figure it all out and say, "That's just one of those things." Or, you can say, "Wow, that's fascinating! I'm going to take charge of my life! I'm going to remain faithful to the One who always has my best interests at heart." It worked for Job!

THE 80/20 RULE

I used to go through a lot of agony, and a lot of anguish, and a lot of sleepless nights just wondering, wondering, wondering. I gave up on all that when I finally understood the 80/20 rule. Let me give some good tips about the 80/20 rule. As a leader, as a manager, as a person who takes charge, being able to influence other people is essential.

Learn to spend 80 percent of your time as a leader with the 20 percent of the people. For maximum efficiency and productivity, this is part of the key to successful leadership. There are plenty of examples that reveal this percentage is correct in various areas of life. It may not be exactly 80/20, but fairly close. For instance, ask the minister of the church, "Who picks up the tab here? How many do most of the work that needs to be done here?" The pastor will probably say, "About 20 percent of the people pick up 80 percent of the tab." This is called "one of those things."

So what do you do? Well, you learn to work with it, not try to solve it. It's like trying to solve the seasons. You can't solve the seasons—you learn to work with the seasons. The seasons—spring, summer, fall, winter—are all set as they are meant to be. Likewise, some things are set by history. The key is to know what can be changed and what is set in place permanently that can't be changed. Then you must learn to work with the way it is set.

So part of the key of leadership is learning to spend 80 percent of your time with the 20 percent of the people who are making the effort, who are doing the 80 percent. That's called good leadership sense.

Work with what can't be changed.

Now you ask, "Well, how do I do that? How exactly does that work?"

Answer: spend individual time with the 20 percent, and spend group time with the 80 percent.

However, guess who wants your individual time? Yep, the 80 percent. The wrong group. But that's what life's all about, right?

Accepting this challenge, you have to be clever, and you have to be diplomatic. *Diplomacy* and *strategy* are two key words to understand to be an effective and take-charge leader.

Here's an example of diplomacy strategy.

Mary comes and says, "I have a question."

You say, "Hi, Mary, bring your question to the meeting Saturday morning. I'm going to meet with everybody, and I'll cover it then."

She says, "Okay."

Now, it might not be quite that easy, but if you put this in perspective now, it will become easy and your time will be better spent. Try to deal with the 80 percent in groups, and then you will have time to talk to the 20 percent individually.

There is always a pull in the opposite direction, always. Gravity is the downward pull. Life is the struggle in the opposite direction of gravity. Life should always be moving upward and forward—the opposite direction of the normal negative.

Someone may say, "Well, I'll just fire the 80 percent. They're only doing 20 percent of the business." Well, I wouldn't fool around with that idea, because after the 80 percent were fired, before too long, whoever is left, 20 percent of them will be doing 80 percent of the business, and 80 percent will be doing 20 percent. Right? This reality is not something you can "fire," it's something you must learn to work with, something you learn to deal with, manage, handle. The 80/20 rule is a very important rule.

LAW OF AVERAGES

There are other tips to understanding ratios, numbers, and categories in this challenge of leadership. The next crucial subject is *the law of averages*. It's important to understand the law of averages in a personal sense and a business sense. Basically, if you do something often enough, you get a ratio of results. It's important for leaders to understand ratios, because if you're working with people in any area of business, you have to have charts to keep track of results—gains and minuses. You must be able to evaluate your own performance as well as their performance.

Ratios. What is meant by ratios? Let's say you're in sales. You join a company and represent the products or the service, and you're first getting started. You talk to ten people. Nine people say, "No, I wouldn't care for any." One says, "Yes, I'll take some." We call this your opening ratio.

One yes out of 10 nos. Depending on what business you're involved with, that may be a good ratio or a poor ratio. You may think that's not a good a ratio, but it all depends on the product or the service. For example, if you are selling luxury vehicles, and one person out of ten buys one and your commission is significant, then one out of ten every day for a week is fantastic.

So this is your opening ratio. At first don't worry about what the numbers are. At first, you're just initiating activity. This very simply is a one out of ten ratio. The very exciting part about dealing in ratios is that once a ratio starts, it tends to continue, to accumulate. When you talk to ten more people, chances are excellent you'll get another yes. If you talk to ten more, chances are excellent you'll get yet another yes. It's uncanny. I don't know how it works, but I know it works. There's a lot of things you don't need to know how they work, just work them.

Some people take time to stop and study the roots of how and why things happen. Others are out there gathering the fruit. You have to decide what end of this law of average thing you want to get in on. It just works. It's a fascinating subject.

Once you have established your ratio, one out of ten, now you can start to compete. It is so important to test your skill against someone else's skill. What someone else can do gives you good insight, a good indication of what can be done. Competition motivates you to stretch what you might be able to do—to reach for the next level of success. Competition is healthy for growth.

Now, you have to be very smart when learning about ratios. Consider this scenario. If you've been with a company for a long time, you may be so good that you can get nine out of ten yeses. Someone, let's call him Jim, who just joined the company can only get one out of ten to say yes. If the company offers a 30-day contest to see who can get the most to say yes to our product or service, even though Jim can only get one out of ten, he will win.

Understanding ratios is key.

You say, "Well, I've been here a long time. I can get nine out of ten to say yes. How could Jim possibly beat me?" It would be very simple.

Now, it might not be easy, but it would be very simple. During the 30 days, since Jim understands ratios, while you talk to ten and get nine, Jim will talk to 100 and get 10; so that at the end of 30 days, you have nine and Jim has 10. He beats you. Isn't that clever?

Let me give you another scenario. If you're new and you're bright, you will make up in numbers what you lack in skill. This is called helping people with the numbers, helping people with ratios. Someone says, "Well, I can only get one out of ten to say yes." You tell that person, "That has nothing to do with competition."

After 30 days, Jim may have been fairly exhausted, but he was pretty good for a 30-day run. The same can work for you.

I have been known not to sleep or eat much during those 30 days. About a four-hour sleep is all I need and about one meal a day, one hour a day for nutrition. I don't recommend or advise you to do the same if you believe your health would become at risk, but if you're the new person, this is a clever way to make up in numbers what you first may lack in skill. You can compete even though you're new. The key is to be bright enough to understand ratios.

TO INCREASE YOUR RATIO

Here's the next tip—ratios can be increased. You talk to ten and get one to say yes; talk to ten more get one; talk to ten more get one; talk to ten more, get two. Why? Why would about the fourth time you talk to ten you get two yeses instead of one? You're getting better!

Key question, who can get better? Answer, anyone who tries. All you have to do is put together the numbers. Your brain is as good as anybody else's. Your chances are as good. All you have to do is find a way to put out the extraordinary effort to do an ordinary thing extremely well. Ratios; success is a numbers game. It's important to keep track of your numbers.

In baseball, keeping track of a players hits is called his batting average. According to *Merriam-Webster Dictionary,* the meaning of batting average is "a ratio (such as a rate per thousand) of base hits to official times at bat for a baseball

Expend extraordinary effort to do something ordinary extremely well.

player." Whatever you're doing, the key is to keep track of your success and how good you are at whatever.

Someone says, "Well, I'm not very good on the telephone." I'll tell you how you can quickly cure all that—start making calls on the telephone. I'm telling you right now—you can get better at anything. All you have to do is attempt it, try it, start putting a string of numbers together, keep track, and understand your own ratios.

THREE SIMPLE STEPS TO A GOOD LIFE AND SUCCESSFUL CAREER

I teach a very simple sales course. Let me give it to you in three points:

1. Talk to lots of people every day.

2. Be very nice.

3. Provide good service.

Number one, talk to lots of people. Isn't that simple? It's a numbers game, especially if you're new—and here's what's exciting, there are lots of people. You don't have to worry about having enough people to talk to, so just talk to as many as possible.

Even if your presentation is poor, if you put the numbers together, something good will happen. Even if your presentation is so poor that you go around every day saying to everybody you meet, "Hi. You wouldn't want to buy anything, would you?" Sure enough somebody will say, "Well, maybe I would. What are you selling?" I'm telling you, it's just about that simple if you put the numbers together. If you talk to lots of people every day, two things will happen. Number one, you're bound to make sales. Some people buy for the strangest reasons. Some people even buy out of sympathy for the salesperson. They don't want to see your kids starve.

If you talk to enough people, somebody will buy. Why? Ratios. Numbers.

I'm certain that you have a much better presentation than saying, "You wouldn't want to buy anything, would you?" I'm sure you can get a little brighter than that. Just start simple. Someone may be asking, "Where do I start?" Start anywhere. It doesn't matter. If you're in sales, walk outside, find a rock, throw it up in the air. Wherever the rock comes down, start right there. That's a good place to start, anywhere.

Then the next person you see, say, "Sir, you're the first man after the rock," and that will definitely get a conversation started. They may back up while they talk, but something will start to happen. This is the reason behind understanding the numbers. You don't have to be so cleverly skillful. All you have to be is bright enough to understand that numbers can make up for lack of skill.

If you're in a leadership position to help people, help them with their ratio. Say to the 20 percent individually, "John, let's go over these numbers one more time. How many calls did you make? Who did you talk to?"

So that's number one, *talk to lots of people every day*. You're bound to get better. You're bound to find someone who wants and needs what you have to offer.

Number two, *be real nice, even when people aren't*. A big part of presentation is attitude, personality, and a sincere smile. People will open their minds and hearts and be receptive to someone who is genuine. Being nice means a pleasant tone and style, one that exudes an agreeable and respectful demeanor. This may be harder when talking with some people over other people; nevertheless, all people deserve to be treated equally.

Number three, *give good service*. Write all the thank-you notes most people don't write. Do all the extra follow-ups most people don't do. Call them before they call you. Good service leads to multiple sales. If you'll take good care of people, they will open doors you could never open yourself. They will take you by the hand and share you with people you never thought you could reach.

That's a simple sales course—that also applies to all walks of life and life itself. Everyone appreciates and responds to nice conversations with someone who is interested in their well-being.

THE SOWER

Our next subject for the study of leadership skills is a fascinating story about the law of averages. The story originates from the Bible (Matthew 13:1-23), and I hope you consider my way of relating the Parable of the Sower to you. My parents made sure by the time I was about 19 that I was a pretty good scholar of the Book, but I'm still an amateur when considering the breadth and depth of all the wisdom within.

A sower in ancient days was simply the person who planted the crops. A sower prepared the ground, got it ready for planting, then with a bag of seed would walk into the field, sowing the seed into the soil.

There are some important points you'll pick up right away when you read the story. First, the sower was a wise man, a great advantage.

Second, he was very ambitious, which is an admirable quality. But ambition has to be tempered or it can become invasive. One writer wrote, "I've learned to be both ambitious and content." That's a unique place to finally arrive, to be both ambitious and content. There is nothing wrong with ambition as long as you work the right formula. The Bible probably gives the greatest formula for wealth and power. It says, if you are faithful over a few things, you will be made ruler over many things. Good philosophy, which teaches us that it is okay to wish to be a ruler. Nothing wrong with that, but here's how you become a good ruler—good stewardship when the amounts are small.

Someone may say, "Oh, if I had a fortune, I'd take good care of it. But I just have a paycheck, so I don't know where the money goes." No, that's not how it works.

I said to Mr. Shoaff when I met him at age 25, "If I had more money, I'd have a better plan."

He said, "Mr. Rohn, I would suggest to you, if you had a better plan you'd have more money."

It's not the amount that counts. It's the philosophy that executes your plan that counts.

If a child has a dollar, what should he do with it? That decision will determine what he does with a dollar for the rest of his life. Someone may say, "Well, it's just a child and it's just a dollar." That attitude is a massive error in judgment. What a colossal mistake in analyzing this scenario.

If a child is allowed to spend the whole dollar without having the sense of where that could take him, that is a great disservice to the child. We must explain the journey he selects when he spends the whole dollar.

So if a child wants to spend the whole dollar, it's best that you say, "No, no, you can't spend the whole dollar."

Child says, "Why not?"

Say, "Well, I'll show you why not." Then take him to the other side of town and say, "Would you like to live here? Here's where the people live who spend all they make. Here's where they live." There's nothing better than visual to illustrate to a child. Show them the tragic circumstances if you spend all you make, if you spend all you have.

Say, "Would you like to live here? Would you like to live like this?"

The kid says, "No, I wouldn't want to live here."

"Then you can't spend the whole dollar."

That kid will come home with big wide eyes. Lesson learned.

Okay, back to my story. Let's review the first two points—the sower was wise and also ambitious. Point three, the sower went to work. It takes activity to furnish the labor that brings new life. Ideas without labor are stillborn—they never become tangible. They never become real. You have to put yourself through the activity, through the labor. So when you read the story, you'll find this was a hardworking sower—an admirable quality.

Point four, the sower had the best seed. It's exciting when you're involved in the best, the best product, the best service, the best idea, the best enterprise, something you feel proud about. That's important in the way you see a situation, to have what you consider the best.

Now with all of these qualities, the sower starts out and now starts to unfold the scenario of life called the law of averages. Here's what happened.

The sower goes out to sow the seeds. The first portion of the seeds that he sows fell by the wayside, and the birds ate it.

I want you to understand the scenario and why it is very important for leaders to engage in teaching the inevitable. Leaders must themselves realize that "birds" are inevitable. Birds will take part of the seed, always, it's inevitable. If you don't teach inevitability, people will be upset when they realize that there will be some seeds that don't bear fruit. If they aren't taught about the "birds," they won't know what to expect. We must be prepared to expect and then handle or deal with what are called eventualities, the inevitable.

So the sower goes out, sowed some of the seeds, and the birds eat it. This is a fairly typical story of life. The birds are going to get some of our seeds.

You may be building an organization. You're out recruiting, and you say, "John, I have an important story for you. Could be a great change of life for you, and chance to earn some extra money, or make it a full-time venture. I hope you'll come Thursday night and take a look."

John says, "Oh, yeah, I think I'm ready for something like that. Thursday night, I'll see you and let's go through it all."

You say, "Wonderful."

It's Thursday night and John isn't there. Where is John?

Setbacks are inevitable but not terminal.

Spend your time wisely—in the field sowing.

The birds got him.

The birds come in a variety of forms. It's called the inevitable. Maybe his brother-in-law said, "Sales? You're not going to get mixed up in sales. Who told you that you were a salesman?" Unfortunately, there are all kinds of statements—true and false—that cause people to back out of a good idea.

When the birds eat away some of your good seed, you have of a couple of choices. One, you can chase away the birds. You say, "Well, I'll go straighten this out." But here's the problem with that decision: if you chase after the birds, you have left the field, and the law of averages isn't going to work for you anymore until you get back to the field.

It is critical to prioritize how you spend your time—what to spend your time on and what not to waste your time on.

There are two ways to have the tallest building in town. One is tear down all the other buildings. Then your building will be the tallest, but we call that the hardest of tasks. You may work to tear down the building right beside yours, and maybe the one on the other side of your building, but the next one may not be that easy. The owner may stand out in front and say, "I've heard about you. I'm not giving in!" Formidable, right? Now you have some problems because you're not known as a builder—you're known as a wrecker, a destroyer. You put others down to make yourself look good. That is a massive error in judgment.

The better and best thing to do when the birds take your seed is to spend your energy and time on what counts, and understand the law of averages. Don't chase the birds, stay in the field.

The story says that the wise sower ignored the birds, and kept on sowing. Why? He was so wise that he understood the law of averages. He knew that if he kept sowing seeds, the chances were very high that some would escape the birds.

So the sower sowed more seeds—some of the seeds fall on rocky ground where the soil was shallow. We call this an inevitability. Sad but true, this is the stuff of life. Those who take charge of their lives realize that there are seasons, ratios, and the inevitable. This is so important, especially as a leader, so you can help people figuring out life and understanding what works, and doesn't work at times. This is called "one of those things."

The parable continues saying that this time the seed takes root and little plants start to grow, but the soil is so shallow that the first hot day the little plants wither and die."

You say, "Wow, what a disappointment."

Well, sure, you're going to be disappointed. Some people are going to try so little even if you have a good idea.

John actually showed up on a Thursday night and chose to join you in your venture. Thirty days later you say, "We had our monthly meeting. John isn't here. Where's John? I thought sure John would last 30 days, but he didn't."

Why? It's called inevitable. Who knows the reason why John didn't show up. Maybe someone said, "Boo," and he quit. First hot day. Now you're disappointed, especially if John was somebody you liked, somebody you knew. But here's what you must learn to do as a leader, this is part of the challenge of life—discipline your disappointment and understand the law of averages.

So what did the wise sower do next? He continued sowing his seeds. How brilliant. He was so well-schooled in the law

Discipline your disappointment.

of averages that he kept sowing. This time the seeds fell on thorny ground and eventually the thorns choke the seedlings to death. What are the thorns of life? The troubles, the angst, who knows the excuses some people use to stop pushing through to get the job done. It's inevitable.

What? You may be wondering, How much ground is there? Is there even enough to get a good crop?

Well, just hang on. It's not the end of the story. But first let's return to missing-in-action John.

Some people try so little. They allow other stuff to crowd out the good opportunities, and who knows why? I don't know why. The key is to take the inevitable and take the obvious and work with it, make it work for your benefit. Everybody should study the obvious, and not let it unduly disturb you; learn to manage the obvious so you can get on with the more important things in life.

I called John and said, "John, where were you last night? We had a meeting."

John says, "Well, I can't make every meeting."

I say, "Why not?"

John says, "Well, I have a lot of other things I need to do."

I ask, "What are the other things?"

You won't believe the list John gave me.

"The backyard fence was sagging, and the dogs were about to get loose. I just can't let my dogs run loose."

I said, "Okay, John."

Then John says, "The screen door came off the hinges, and I just can't let things fall apart. I have to take time, and keep things fixed up."

154

I said, "Okay, John."

"Some extra trash had piled up in the garage. I just can't let mountains of trash take over. I got to take care of the trash."

I said, "Okay, John." While listening to him on the phone, I could almost hear the thorns choking him right out of a good opportunity.

Some people have the incredible ability to major in minor things. I don't know why. We call this the inevitable. We call it a mystery. It's part of the scenario of life.

Later that week I was driving through our little community and saw John out there mowing his lawn. He's cussing the weeds, he's red in the face, and he's about to explode. I said, "John, what are you doing?"

He says, "What does it look like? I'm mowing this lousy lawn."

I said, "John, there are lots of neighborhood boys around here who can mow your lawn."

He says, "They want $5. I'll mow it myself!"

Okay, John. Okay. There should be a law against cheating some young neighborhood boy out of $5.

But back to the story of the sower, which is told to prepare us for the inevitable called the law of averages.

The sower continued to sow—evidently knowing the law of averages and how the more he sowed, the more chances he had for the seeds to take root and be fruitful. No matter that the bird ate some seeds and the sun baked some seeds and some thorns choked some seeds, he was determined to sow more seeds. He wasn't going to let little things cheat him out of big chances. He understood inevitabilities. He kept sowing.

If you share a good idea often enough, it will fall on good people.

The next part of the parable tells us that the seeds fell on good ground. Let me give you a promise as a leader. Good seed will always, eventually, fall on good ground. Key phrase— if you share a good idea often enough, it'll fall on good people. Why? The law of averages.

Now, even the good ground had a variety of productivity. The parable says that some seed fell on good soil where it produced a crop—a hundred, sixty, or thirty times what was sown! That's the law of averages. That's the way it is. It's called "one of those things."

Now, can you find some 100 percenters who will take advantage of your offer of opportunity? The answer is yes, but you may have to go through the birds, the hot weather, the thorns and cares, and you may have to find some way to use the 30 percenters and the 60 percenters. And when you become entrusted as a skillful leader, learn the law of averages, and learn how to deal with all the stuff of life, and know you will definitely have some 100 percenters to work with to share your success. The law of averages.

7

LEADERS
TAKE CHARGE

As leaders, let's learn to help people not just with their jobs but with their lives. I think we have a twofold responsibility to help people with job skills, but I think the greater responsibility is to help people with life skills. Let's not just teach people how to work. Let's teach people how to live. How to assimilate and accumulate far greater treasures than just a paycheck. The treasures of awareness, understanding, setting goals, reaching into the future, growing, changing, and expanding.

Let's talk about team building with our new understanding and background of the law of averages. I can give you some good scenarios about putting a good team together, looking for good people. Building a championship team and building a successful team of people to accomplish a worthwhile purpose can be challenging as well as very satisfying. Whatever your endeavor, whether an enterprise or an organization, or whether it's church or sports, no matter the plan you have in mind, if you want to find good people, it is possible. This last chapter discusses how to meet the challenges of finding a successful team of people.

The key is not to become discouraged along the way. People come in all shapes and sizes with a multitude of perspectives, goals, beliefs, and backgrounds. Every selection may not work out. After all, even Jesus picked Judas.

To put together a good team, I offer the following checklist with five parts to help.

Number one, history. It's a good idea to check people's employment history and qualifications to do the job excellently. Don't just skim over their resume; take a good look.

Number two, is the person genuinely interested. Sometimes people fake their interest. A face-to-face interview is the best way to determine the person's interest and desire to be on your team. If you've been a leader for a while, you are probably a good judge of character after having a more-then-superficial conversation with a potential team member.

Number three, response. A person's response tells you a lot about his or her integrity, character, personality, interests, and skills. Warning signs include someone asking early on in the interview, "Do I have to stay late? Is the break only 10 minutes? Do I have to work Saturdays?" Don't overlook these warning signs. A person's response quickly illustrates their philosophy. People respond based on what they know. Their attitude and philosophy is ingrained and they might be clever for a while, but their natural response will eventually emerge during an interactive conversation. Be aware of any discrepancies you see in demeanor, oral, and written responses.

Number four, results. Ask about past results, the person's track record in previous employment situation. Results are how we judge performance. If the person has passed the first three criteria and is hired, results must soon match quality. He or she might be a nice person, but you have to have good results for the effort. There are two parts to results: One, activity results. Sometimes we don't ask for productivity right away, all we ask for first is activity. It's pretty easy to check activity. If you joined a sales organization and you're supposed to make ten calls the first week, it's simple to check on Friday.

"John, how many calls did you make this week?"

John starts telling an excuse story and you say, "John, I don't need a story, I just need an activity number from one to ten." If the activity results from the first week are not good, that should prompt you to review the numbers again after another week. You have to be the judge how much time you allow for someone's lack of precise activity.

Number five, productivity. Finally, the ultimate test of a quality team is productivity. Fruit, evidence, measurable progress in reasonable time.

As a leader, a leadership skill you have to learn is how to measure results and productivity and activity. Be up front about what you expect when team building. People don't like surprises when it comes to their job. Be up front with people. God was very up front. In the Old Testament, God says, "If you move toward Me, I move toward you." That's making His position clear. You must make your position clear as well. I take a step, I expect you to take a step—then each team member knows how it works. Also, "If you don't move, I don't move."

You may say, "Well, that's arbitrary." Well, as the leader you have that prerogative. You can set up your policies and procedures that way. A good philosophical statement: Life was designed to respond to deserve, not to need. On this planet

Life was designed to respond to deserve, not to need.

life's slogan doesn't read, "If you need, you will reap." No. It reads, "If you plant, you will reap." You say, "Well, I really need to reap." Then you really need to plant. Life wasn't designed for the needers. Life was designed for the planters.

Life doesn't respond to what we need. Life responds to what we deserve by activity, belief, faith, action, movement. You have to take a step.

It's important to make clear when you bring somebody on board that they have a responsibility and commitment to be an active member of the team. You may want to say something such as, "Mary, if you step out and do _____, we will do _____ in return for you. If you take three steps in the direction of _____, we will do this, this, and this. But if you don't move, we don't move." It's very important to make it clear that taking action, exhibiting initiative, and being motivated is what gets noticed and moves them forward. Why? Because everybody needs to work toward the goal. Life responds to deserve, not need.

Another leadership skill is to work with the people who deserve it, not the people who need it. This applies to team building now. We're talking about winning a championship. We're talking putting together an enterprise. And the key to leadership is to teach people how to deserve it. Teach them how to take the steps necessary, teach them how to make the moves to advance the goal. We ask for activity, for steps in the right direction. Without taking steps, there is no promise, no reward at the end because you never reach the end, accomplish your goal, attain the prize, fulfill your purpose, or claim your full potential.

So this is one of the most important things you can teach children as well—how to earn and deserve good things, how

Learn to work with people who deserve it, not people who need it.

to earn and deserve the favors. You have to pay the price by taking the required action—that's how you deserve it.

Another next key in building a successful team is to realize when you have too many team members. A simple but good example of this key is a story that again comes from the Bible.

When facing a very large army, the good Lord told His guy, Gideon, twice, "You have too many soldiers." The first time 22,000 men left while 10,000 men remained. The second time all but 300 men remained to fight. Can you guess the outcome?

The following narrative isn't exactly how it's stated in the book of Judges chapter 7, but it's very close and you'll understand the point I'm making.

God told Gideon to give the 32,000 soldiers a pep talk before going into battle. Gideon was to tell the men that they would soon be off to fight, and if anybody was afraid and thought the army was going to lose this battle upcoming with the Midianites, they should go home and not fight this time. They were excused.

Gideon waits, and sure enough some went home; in fact, 22,000 soldiers left the camp. If he

had 32,000 men and 22,000 thought they were going to lose, guess what? They were going to lose. There were too many.

In haste to build a team, it's possible to recruit losers. It doesn't mean it's wrong, it just means it's possible—it's just "one of those things." When you're making moves, sometimes there's no telling who you may collect along the way who isn't fully on board.

It's just one of those things.

So here's a tip: during the interview or probation period, ask outright something such as, "Do you believe that this project—idea, business, plan, enterprise, etc.—is going to win or lose? What is your honest opinion?" If you don't hear a positive or convincing response, say, "You can be excused."

So Gideon has 10,000 soldiers left. He says, "No problem. We'll fight the battle with 10,000." The good Lord says, "Well, you still have too many." Gideon says, "What?" And the good Lord says, "March the 10,000 till they're hot and thirsty down by the river and those who are careless will drop their shield and spear and dive in the water and start drinking, you can't use them. They're too reckless. But the ones who keep their spears and the shields and lap the water like a dog and keep looking and alert—those are the ones who are trained and ready to go into battle and win."

Gideon said, "Clever." And he marched the 10,000 soldiers down to the river, and they were hot and thirsty. Sure enough, 9,700 men were so hot they became careless and threw down their spears and shields and jumped into the river to drink the cool water. The remaining 300 got down on their knees to drink while holding on to their spears and shields.

Again, in haste, it's possible to recruit the careless. It doesn't mean it's wrong, it just means it's inevitable, it's just "one of those things." If you have an important battle, and crucial encounter, you have to know who's careless.

So Gideon says, "You 9,700, go home." And he sent them home, dripping wet. Now he has 300 soldiers left. Gideon said, "No problem." From 32,000 to 300 fighting men, Gideon is still willing to try it. That's courageous leadership! You have to read the story—it's fascinating.

To the uncommitted and careless, "Go home."

With only 300 to fight against thousands, the battle plan was the most strange and unusual strategy ever designed. But he won the day and chased off the Midianites. Gideon became a military hero. His story provides a leadership lesson: there are times when you may have too many members—weed out the ones who are not 100 percent on board and the ones who are careless and reckless. Having uncommitted team members is inevitable. Next, don't linger too long in sending them home. When you have a job to do, be fairly swift in your analysis of who will and who won't and who can and who can't.

Jesus said to His twelve, in putting the Christian philosophy to work, that they should go out into the cities sharing the story of the good news with the people. And if they respond fairly soon, stay. But if they don't respond fairly soon, don't stay. He advised them to leave the city that didn't respond fairly soon (see Matthew 10:5-14).

You have to be the judge of how much time you give someone to respond or something to respond. This is part of the unusual skill of leadership, learning time dimensions, how much time to give someone or something who seems not to be a good fit. Jesus was fairly clear when telling them not to stay too long. If the city doesn't accept the story, He said to leave. And I think the reason was fairly clear—there are many cities who will want to hear the good news, so they shouldn't linger with those who don't.

It goes back to the law of averages. Play the law of averages. Don't stay too long with those who won't join in 100 percent—go find those who will.

He gave the guys some other fascinating instructions that when they walk out of one of the cities that doesn't accept the story, they should "shake off the dust from your feet." Whatever that meant in those days. One meaning of the phrase is that if a place refuses to welcome you or listen to you, shake its dust from your feet as you leave to show that you have abandoned those people to their fate.[1]

I believe that leaders must have a sense of timing regarding measurable progress. You have to be smart enough to measure progress and you have to also be smart enough to understand the difference between reasonable and unreasonable timing. The enterprise may be lost for lingering too long, not understanding the law of averages.

GOOD AND EVIL

Leaders must understand the fact that there is both good and evil in the world. It's part of the life scenario to understand good and evil—however you wish to describe good and however you wish to frame your ideology of evil. There are a variety of ways to describe these two opposing forces. For some people, evil is too strong a word. I don't know why, but it's part of their personal aversions.

Good and evil are part of your own philosophical conclusions when trying to evaluate this earthly struggle. Evil, good, tyranny, liberty, sickness, health, winning, losing, life, death, opportunity, tragedy, and much more are all part of the life scenario. Much of life is described in rather philosophical terms on a higher plane called the great war between good and evil.

Now, here's part of the scenario. When the founding fathers put together the United States of America, they said,

Accept that life includes both good and evil.

in essence, "We want maximum liberty and minimum law. We have to have laws to restrain that mysterious dark side of our nature. Because sure enough, even though we have a good thing going here in America, there are probably some people who are not going to run by the rules. So not only will we build some cities, we probably better build some jails."

Why would they consider all that? They were bright enough to understand this clash, this scenario of good and evil. And all good leaders must understand this clash, this scenario, however you wish to describe it. Whatever terms you wish to call it, we must understand that it is reality.

Part of that understanding is to acknowledge that some people have sold out to the evil side, for whatever reason. You don't have to spend much time with why; all you have to do is spend time with *who* to come to a conclusion.

HERE AND GONE

I went to my 30th year class reunion a few years ago, held in the small village where I grew up. There were only about 150 in the graduating class and after 30 years, about half of the class attended the reunion, which I thought was a pretty good turnout. We had a two-day celebration. I was the master of ceremonies.

On the second day, we had a little moment to remember the classmates who were now deceased. I think there were eight and I knew them all, so I gave a little scenario, a little story about each one. Then we took time, just a brief moment of silence to remember, because some were very unique human beings, but now they were gone.

I thought later, *Eight out of 150 after 30 years, is that about average?* Guess what I discovered? It *is* about average. So

Not if but when...

after 30 years out of 150, the question isn't *will* eight be missing, the question is *who* will be missing?

So part of the scenario of understanding leadership is to not be surprised when the inevitable occurs. If you are too surprised by the inevitable, you are called naive. For example, when the sun goes down one evening and someone says, "What happened? Where's the sun?" That someone is naive. There are just some things you don't want to be surprised about, especially in public.

Remember John from a previous chapter? He's the guy who said yes he would show up Thursday night for the meeting, but he was a no-show. And when you cornered him about why, he gave you a long list of various excuses. If you ask, "Why did John do that? Why did he say he'd attend the meeting and then not show up? Why did he give me all those excuses?" If you keep asking those same questions over and over as if you're surprised, you are being naïve.

John is a very mild case of going over to the "other side." Still, it's very sobering as to why some have chosen to give themselves over to being untruthful, deceptive, even evil. We call it simply "one of those things."

Another key to effective leadership is to understand and be alert and bright enough to spot deception and unethical behavior and deal with it up front and quickly. An excellent example that all good leaders must understand is the story of the frog and the scorpion. It's one of the most important stories for a leader to keep in the back of their minds when dealing with typical humans and their complicated makeup.

A FROG AND A SCORPION

A frog and a scorpion appeared on the bank of a river about the same time. The frog was about to jump in the river and swim to the other side. And along comes the scorpion and sees that the frog is about to swim across the river. So the scorpion engages the frog in conversation, saying, "Mr. Frog, I see that you're about to jump in the river and swim to the other side."

And the frog says to the scorpion, "That is correct."

The scorpion says, "Hey, hey, hold on. I would like to get to the other side, but unfortunately I'm a scorpion and I can't swim. Would you be so kind just to let me hop on your back and you swim across the river and deposit me on the other side? I would be grateful."

The frog looked at the scorpion and said, "No way! You're a scorpion and scorpions sting frogs and kill them. I'd get out there halfway with you on my back and you'd sting me and I'd die. You think I'm crazy? No way."

The scorpion said, "Hey, hold it with your frog brain, you're not thinking. If I was to sting you out there halfway, sure you'd die and drown, but so would I since I'm a scorpion and I can't swim. That'd be kind of foolish. So I'm not about to do that. I just want to get to the other side."

The frog thought over that reasoning and said, "That makes sense. Hop on."

And according to the story, the scorpion hops on the frog's back. They start across the river and sure enough, halfway across the river, the scorpion stings the frog. They are now both about to go down for the third time. The frog can't believe what happened and he says to the scorpion, "Why did you do that? I'm about to die and drown, but so are you. Why would you do that?"

And the scorpion said, "Because I am a scorpion."

Likewise, some people's human nature—good or evil—is so ingrained and so deeply rooted that they are the way they will always be. Leaders must understand the story of the frog and the scorpion. Another analogy: there are shepherds and there are sheep and there are wolves. Wise leaders must realize that some "wolves" are so clever they have learned to dress up like sheep. Be aware of people who seem as gentle as sheep but underneath may be vicious.

Life consists of the full-drama struggle between good and evil. And it's all part of the test of leadership skill, awareness, sensitivity, understanding, knowing the scenario and being on the alert for what is called the inevitable.

ENGAGING LEADERSHIP STUDIES

There are several studies that leaders should engage in, studies helpful in taking charge of your life and unlocking influence, wealth, and power—and making the most of yourself. This list and the descriptions are not exhaustive, but you can easily expand on each one in your own good time and in your own good way. The list of studies in which leaders should engage: possibility, opportunity, ability, inevitability, rationality.

POSSIBILITY

Number one is the study of possibility. The possibilities for leaders to experience are endless. For example, it's fun to play the "What if" game to explore opportunities and possibilities. Ask yourself: "What if I had enough people? What if I had refined people? What if I had effective leaders? What if I had a great team? What if I took my product/service to the market? What if I accomplished my current and all my future goals? What if I could live my dream? What are the dimensions? What's the size? What's the promise? What's the reward?"

Possibilities are all around us. We must all be students of possibility. Dr. Schuller calls it possibility thinking. It's not a bad subject for study, possibilities.

OPPORTUNITY

Leaders must always be conscious and aware of the expanded potential for opportunities. Sometimes, if not most of the time, an opportunity is closer than you think. Opportunities come in diverse ways—be on the lookout for unusual or unique opportunities that will move your business or venture in a different direction, a better location, a wiser investment, etc. Opportunities may be presented by a friend, colleague, teacher, pastor, acquaintance, or someone you meet at an event. Keep an open mind regarding opportunities.

ABILITY

The next subject of study is ability. Leaders must be good students of honing their own abilities, as well as recognizing the ability of others. Sometimes it's easy to overlook someone's exceptional abilities who is right close to you. You never took time to notice all of their talent and their potential. Someone who works for or with you may have hidden skills that need to be brought to light and used to your and their benefit.

I discovered a young man in Canada who worked for the railroad. He was making about $300 a month and had been working there ten years. (This was a long time ago.) He became a good friend of mine and I recruited him and he joined my company, my business. The second year he was with me he made $45,000. Now he's a leader in the community, he's gifted and skillful, financially independent, and he's a unique gentleman.

The railroad had him for ten years, but they didn't uncover his ability—they didn't know who they had. They didn't have an in-depth survey or process to find the people who were already employees who may have had some unusual gifts, capabilities, and capacities that hadn't been discovered. So leaders must learn how to expose ability and put in place ways to uncover hidden ability that may have been there for a while but not used. Find a way to bring to the surface all that each person, employee, team member, etc. has to offer—that's good leadership. The same is true of your family, especially your children. Help bring their potential to the fullest, their skills and talents to the forefront.

INEVITABILITY

All of us should be students of inevitability. We should routinely ask ourselves, "Without kidding myself, if I keep up my current daily practices, where will it take me in ten years without being disillusioned? I don't want to just cross my fingers and walk the wrong road. How can I learn to look into the future called inevitable and use it to my advantage?"

Inevitability is being 200 feet from Niagara Falls in a little boat with no motor and no oars. The end result of that scenario is inevitable—it's over. What a tragic place to find yourself. If someone had painted you this scene when you were still upstream, painted the roar of the falls in your mind and showed you what a tragic place you were headed toward—you might not have drifted so far into the inevitable.

We have to help people by painting the roar of the falls long before they get 200 feet in a little boat with no motor and no oars. Someone says, "Well, the roar of the falls is a long way off." Yes, but the people who are around you are drifting, drifting, and with leadership perception you have to see where they are heading and you have to level with them and speak the truth—give them alternate choices while there are still alternate choices for them to make. This is the gift of leadership.

Leadership that takes charge helps people avoid the negative inevitabilities during life changes, career changes, family changes, thinking and attitude changes, life and death changes—and helping people see all the possible positive inevitabilities.

RATIONALITY

Another great subject for leaders to study is rationality—being able to rightly conclude based on information, a rational and sensible course. Good tip—make sure what you conclude is the product of your own conclusion. Take advice, but not orders. Let others around you be helpful, but then put what you came up with through your own mental computer and make sure that is the product of what you concluded based on all the input. We call this a true sense of leadership, developing rationality based on credible information.

CHALLENGES

Taking charge of your life and being a leader who takes charge are not easy tasks, but they are worthy tasks that are possible. You are walking the summit of leadership skills, and most people don't want to take the time and effort to engage in these extra and necessary disciplines. But I promise you that the treasure and the equity is so tremendous that what price is paid in these early disciplines is very small compared to the treasure that accumulates as the days unfold—for your heart and your mind and your wallet.

To finish and wrap up all of what I've shared with you, I leave you with some good challenges for you to consider.

Here's the first one. *Deal in what matters, what's important in life, the largeness of responsibility and helping others*. Let other people lead small lives, not you. Let others cry over small hurts, not you. Let everyone else argue over non-essentials, not you. Step up to the responsibility and the opportunity to touch people's lives with hope and positivity, to help give others light and direction and refinement of thought and character and activity, potential, opportunity, dreams, and price. Be part of the larger challenge, the larger opportunity.

Here's my next challenge. As a take-charge leader, *help people not just with their jobs but with their lives*. I think we have a twofold responsibility to help people with job skills, but I think the greater responsibility is to help people with life skills. Let's not only teach people how to work, let's teach people how to live. How to assimilate and accumulate far greater treasures than just a paycheck. The treasures of awareness, understanding, setting goals, reaching into the future, growing, changing, expanding.

When we touch people's lives as well as their skills, and if they stay with us a week or a month or a year or a lifetime, on whatever occasion they should choose to leave, we want them to leave by saying, "My experience with you was the greatest experience of my life and it wasn't just what I *earned,* it was what I *learned."*

And the last challenge, *do your best with your gifts—your mind, heart, and soul.* An ancient scenario comes from the Bible and says, "If you work on your gifts, they will make room for you." In other words, if you use your gifts, your gifts will make a place for you, a place of leadership, a place of influence, a place to touch someone else's life in a good way, to make a mark in the world, to further an enterprise, to build a dream. And someday, if you share your gifts to the benefit of others, you will be called noble.

You may receive rewards you can't even now imagine. Plaques to hang on your wall, trophies to sit on the shelf—but most of all, the gift of knowing yourself. That you did the best you could with what you had, the expansion of your mind and your heart, and your soul and your touch and your reach and all the gifts that you possess. Your gifts—if you work on sharing them with others, others will make room for you.

I have to admit to being one of the better examples of all that advice. Look where my gifts have brought me. I was raised in obscurity, in a small village in Idaho. I now get to travel around the world. My gifts have brought me to many rooms in various prestigious venues and what an exciting experience it is for me share myself with others. One of the most challenging, and rewarding, experiences in life is seeing what you can do to help someone else.

One of the greatest thrills in life is to invest life into life. And I've been blessed to have that opportunity over and over. Through this book I've invested a bit of my life into your life, and I've considered it worth it. I thank you for giving me this chance and this opportunity. I wish you leadership. I wish you influence. I wish you treasures of the soul and the spirit and the mind and the wallet, and hopefully what I've had to share with you has given you a sense of extra perception in sharpening your skills and making your life unique.

Now go influence people with your wisdom, compassion, and leadership capabilities, sharing all you have for their benefit—fulfilling your ultimate potential and destiny.

Thank you.

NOTE

1. https://www.bibleref.com/Mark/6/Mark-6-11.html; accessed July 25, 2023.

ABOUT JIM ROHN
(1930-2009)

For more than 40 years, Jim Rohn honed his craft like a skilled artist—helping people the world over sculpt life strategies that expanded their imagination of what is possible. Those who had the privilege of hearing him speak can attest to the elegance and common sense of his material.

So, it is no coincidence that he is still widely regarded as one of the most influential thinkers of our time, and thought of by many as a national treasure. He authored numerous books and audio and video programs and helped motivate and shape an entire generation of personal-development trainers and hundreds of executives from America's top corporations.

THANK YOU FOR READING THIS BOOK!

If you found any of the information helpful, please take a few minutes and leave a review on the bookselling platform of your choice.

BONUS GIFT!

Don't forget to sign up to try our newsletter and grab your free personal development ebook here:

soundwisdom.com/classics

Embark on a transformative journey with Jim Rohn's *The Art of Exceptional Living*. This succinct guide, segmented into focused chapters, offers invaluable insights on personal development, goal setting, and forging a unique path in life. Rohn, with his personal and often humorous anecdotes, encourages readers to evaluate their lifestyles, urging them to become the best versions of themselves. A book that promises not just wealth, but an enrichment of life's value, steering you towards a fulfilling path of self-betterment and happiness. Start living exceptionally today with Rohn's profound wisdom.

Discover the transformative power of true ambition with Jim Rohn's groundbreaking book, *The Power of Ambition*. Rohn, a revered authority on success, guides you on a path to harnessing your innermost drive to foster personal achievement and uplift those around you. Through six pioneering strategies, you'll learn to cultivate a disciplined and eager desire that propels you toward your goals while serving others. From mastering resilience to effective networking, this comprehensive guide is a masterclass in building a life filled with passion and purpose.

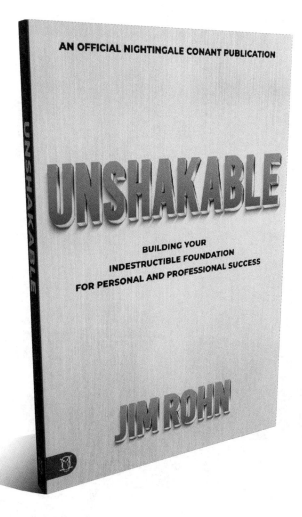

Unlock your potential and pave the road to personal and professional success with *Unshakable*, the famous tour de force from the distinguished Jim Rohn. Drawing from over four decades of insights into human behavior, Rohn presents twelve fundamental qualities to forge an unshakable character that magnetizes success. With captivating insights and actionable strategies, it's your indispensable companion in crafting a rewarding future grounded in steadfast principles. Take the first step towards becoming *Unshakable* — a version of yourself that is grounded, resilient, and primed for success in all life's avenues.